ALLEGHENY INTERMEDIATE UNIT
SUNRISE SCHOOL
550 AURA DRIVE
MONROEVILLE, PA 15146

W9-BMA-412

Corrective Reading

SRA
Decoding Strategies

Decoding B2

Siegfried Engelmann
Gary Johnson
Linda Carnine
Linda Meyer
Wesley Becker
Julie Eisele

 SRA

Columbus, OH

SRAonline.com

 SRA

Send all inquiries to this address:
SRA/McGraw-Hill
4400 Easton Commons
Columbus, OH 43219

ISBN: 978-0-07-611226-5
MHID: 0-07-611226-8

12 13 14 QVR/LEH 13 12 11

The **McGraw·Hill** Companies

Contents

1 f<u>ir</u>st pr<u>ou</u>d g<u>a</u>rden blu<u>sh</u>ed b<u>ea</u>t

2 <u>b</u>irds <u>h</u>ard <u>cl</u>oud t<u>ea</u>rs l<u>ea</u>ving <u>our</u>

3

A	B	C	D
gr<u>i</u>p	t<u>i</u>m	s<u>i</u>te	c<u>o</u>ne
gr<u>i</u>pe	t<u>i</u>me	s<u>i</u>t	con

4 <u>close</u> <u>choked</u> <u>powerful</u> <u>right</u> <u>stared</u>

taking these whiff stinker low

flying risks you're skunks

noses why talked done nobody

said striped taken turn

5

Five Stink Bugs Have a Contest

There were five stink bugs that lived in a garden. Stink bugs   12
are proud if they can make a big stink. The biggest stink bug in   26
the garden was very proud. She said, "This is how to make a   39
stink." And she made a big stink that you could smell on the   52
other side of the garden.   57

The fattest stink bug said, "If you think that her stink is so   70
hot, look at what I can do." The fattest bug gave out with a   84
smell that filled the air <u>for</u> three blocks.   92

The other bugs held their noses. They said, "That was as 103
good a stink as we have smelled for some time." 113

[1]

The next stink bug had a striped back. He said, "If a bug has 127
stripes on its back, it has the best stinker. Here I go." And there 141
he went. 143

A stink came from him and fell like a cloud on the other 156
bugs. They rubbed their eyes. They said, "If the air does not 168
clear soon, we will pass out." 174

A bird was flying over the garden. She looked at the stink 186
bugs in the garden and said, "What are you bugs doing? Don't 198
you think that you'd better stop stinking? Remember there are 208
others who have to smell your stink, too." 216

[1]

"Stop talking," the striped stink bug said to the bird. "Can't 227
you see that we are seeing who has the best stinker?" 238

The bird said, "Yes, I can see that. And I can smell that, 251
too." The bird left. 255

The next stink bug said, "I'll bet that I can beat the rest of 269
you in making a stink." So that bug began to make a stink. It 283
was so bad that the other bugs choked. The biggest bug said, 295
"Ugh! That was some stink!" 300

A rabbit at the other end of the garden called out, "So far as 314
I can tell, you all smell the same. And that's bad. I have tears in 329
my eyes. I cannot see. So I ask you, please, stop stinking." 341

[2]

"Stop talking," the biggest bug said to the rabbit. "We can't 352
take time from our stink meet to talk to you. We are in the 366
middle of something big." 370

The last stink bug was the smallest of all. She had spots on
her back. She said, "Now that the rest of you are done, let me
tell you about the stink that I'll make. Don't come too close
when I begin stinking, or you will get so bent out of shape that
you will never be the same. Nobody can stand the smell that I
make."

[1]

The smallest stink bug kept talking. She said, "In the last
garden I was at, I took the first prize for stinking. I have taken
more prizes for stinking than all of the stink bugs in this land.
When I let go, my stink will lay you low."

The fattest stink bug said, "You're doing a lot of talking, but
you're not doing much stinking. If you came to stink, start
stinking and stop talking."

The smallest bug stared at the fattest bug. She said, "All
right, I'll give out with my stink, but soon you will know why I
told you about it before I let it go. You will see why I took time
to tell you what it would do. When you are choking in the
grass, you'll wish that I had made you leave the garden."

[2]

The striped bug said, "I'm not taking any risks. Any bug
who talks like that must have some kind of stinker." So the
striped bug left.

The little bug kept talking. She said, "One time, I made a
stink that was so powerful it turned all the grass brown. I'll bet
that I can beat ten skunks in a stinking contest."

The fattest bug said, "I came here for a stinking meet, not a
talking meet. I'm leaving." And he did. The little bug kept
talking. Soon another bug left.

[1]

1

call high waiting fort

salt sore night forest

2

about breathed third bald

card fainting feared smallest

3

A	B	C	D
robe	rat	ride	hop
rob	rate	rid	hope

4

laugh burn straight die

wouldn't choke closed

knocks ready shown bet

taken deeply tired our

afraid turn stinks

5

The Little Bug Wins the Meet

There was a contest in the garden. Five stink bugs were   11
trying to see who had the best stinker. All of the bugs but one   25
had shown off their best stink. Now that bug began telling the   37
others how good she was at stinking. She talked and talked.   48
The other bugs began to leave. Now only the biggest bug   59
was left.   61

The little bug with spots said, "If you wish, I will give you a 75
very small stink. My smallest stink will choke you up for three 87
hours. Would <u>you</u> like me to do that? Or would you like me to 101
give the stink of stinks?" 106

[1]

"I'm getting tired of waiting," the biggest bug said. "No stink 117
can be as good as you say your stink is." 127

The little bug said, "Then you're set for my stink? Breathe in 139
deeply and hold in the air, for here it comes." 149

"No, wait," the biggest bug said. "Maybe I'd better go to the 161
other side of the garden. I'll stand there, and I'll be able to get 175
a better whiff of your stink." 181

The biggest bug was afraid. She feared that the smell would 192
do her in. So she went to the other side of the garden. 205

[1]

The little bug asked, "Have you taken a big gulp of air?" 217
"Yes," the biggest bug said. 222
"Are your eyes closed?" 226
"Why should I close my eyes?" the biggest bug asked. 236
"My stink will burn your eyes so badly that you will not see 249
straight for three days. My stink is so powerful that even bats 261
get sore eyes when I turn on my stinker." 270

The biggest bug closed her eyes and breathed in deeply. Then 281
she said, "I'm all set." 286

The little bug asked, "Are you grabbing onto something? 295
Nobody can stand up when my stink reaches them. First it hits 307
them so hard that they fall down. Then it knocks the air from 320
them. And when it has done that, my stink chokes them up. But 333
most bugs don't die from the smell. They are just sick for weeks." 346

[2]

The biggest bug said, "Wait. I'm not ready. I think I'll back 358
up a little more." 362

"Tell me when you're ready," the little bug said. "I'll count to 374
ten, and then I'll turn on my stinker." 382

"All right," the biggest bug said, and that bug began to run. 394
She ran so fast that the grass bent down as she went past. She 408
ran up the hill on the other side of the garden. She didn't turn 422
back. She didn't call to the bug. She just ran. 432

The little bug said, "That big stink bug can really run." Then 444
the little bug began to laugh. That bug laughed so loud that a 457
bird came to see who was making all the loud sounds. 468

[2]

"Why are you laughing so hard?" the bird asked. 477

Soon the bug stopped laughing. The bug said, "I'm laughing 487
because I got rid of all those stink bugs." 496

"I'm glad of that," the bird said. "Where there are stink 507
bugs, there is a lot of stink. I hate stink bugs." 518

"Me, too," said the little bug. 524

"Why should you hate stink bugs? You're one of them." 534

The little bug said, "I'm not one of them. I would never make 547
a stink." 549

"Why wouldn't you make a stink?" the bird asked. 558

The little bug went, "Ho, ho." Then she said, "Because I am 570
a lady bug." 573

[2]

1 ea<u>ch</u>   <u>f</u>old   <u>c</u>oa<u>ch</u>   w<u>ou</u>ld

2 <u>r</u>aised   thir<u>teen</u>   green<u>h</u>ou<u>s</u>e   sma<u>ll</u>er

blu<u>sh</u>ed   <u>s</u>tar<u>t</u>ed   <u>al</u>ways   br<u>ee</u>d   swin<u>g</u>

3

A	B	C	D
sl<u>o</u>pe	m<u>a</u>de	c<u>o</u>p	p<u>i</u>n
sl<u>o</u>p	m<u>a</u>d	c<u>o</u>pe	p<u>i</u>ne

4 <u>studied</u>   <u>botany</u>   skim   basket

checks   pond   clod   tried

5 fellow   blade   hang   fifteen

lonely   dribble   smile   block   grow

school   stuck   nothing   skipping

shy   stared   stayed   flowers   two

grown   Patty   along   show   laugh

burn   different   front   shoot   walked

6   Lonely Art

Art was a farm boy. He talked like a farm boy. He walked   13
like a farm boy. And when he was thirteen years old, he began   26
to grow. When he was fifteen years old, he was taller than any   39
other kid. His arms seemed too long. He looked like a long   51
blade of grass.   54

After school, he didn't hang out with the other kids in his   66
class. He went home to work on the farm. The other kids in his   80
class said, "Art's a loner. He never hangs out <u>with</u> us." They   92
didn't know that Art was shy.   98

[1]

A teacher in the school told Art that he should go out for   111
basketball. And Art did. But he hadn't played basketball   120
before. And he wasn't any good. He couldn't shoot the ball. He   132
couldn't block shots. He couldn't dribble the ball.   140

The coach said, "Art, this game is too hard for you. Why   152
don't you try out for another sport?"   159

But Art didn't try another sport. After school, he went down   170
to the pond near his farm house. He skipped stones on the   182
pond. He said to himself, "I just wish there were a   193
stone-skipping team. I'd be the champ of that team."   202

[1]

Art could skip stones across the water like nothing you have   213
ever seen. He could make the stones turn to the left or turn to   227
the right. He could make them skip way up into the air. Or he   241
could make them skim along the water. And if he took a big   254
swing, he could make a stone skip almost to the other side of   267
the pond.   269

But there was no stone-skipping team, and Art didn't have   279
much fun in school that fall. He felt like a big clod. He felt that   294
the other kids had a lot of fun, but he didn't fit into their plans.   309
Art would smile and try to talk with them. But he didn't know   322
what to talk about, and they didn't seem to want to talk.   334
[2]

Then, in the winter, things were different. Patty came to   344
Art's school. She was in two of Art's classes. One class was   356
botany. Art tried to think of botany when he sat in that class,   369
but Patty sat right in front of him. And every time he looked at   383
Patty, he stopped thinking about botany and started to think   393
about Patty.   395

One of the things they studied in botany was flowers. Art   406
raised roses in his dad's greenhouse. So Art took some roses to   418
school one day. He was going to show them to the class. One of   432
them was a breed that Art's dad had grown.   441
[1]

Some of the boys saw Art going to class with the roses.   453
"What are you going to do with those flowers, Art? Give them   465
to Patty?"   467

In class, Art showed the roses to the teacher and the other   479
kids. The teacher asked Art to tell about growing roses. So Art   491
did. But he didn't give a very good talk. He kept looking at   504
Patty.   505

When the class was over, Patty came up to him. She said,   517
"That was a very good talk, Art." She had never said much to   530
Art before, and Art felt funny talking to her. All of the other   543
kids were looking at him.   548
[2]

Patty said, "Those are very pretty roses. What are you going 559
to do with them?" 563

"I don't know," Art said. 568

"May I have one of them?" she asked. 576

Art blushed. "Yes, you can, Patty," he said. His cheeks felt 587
hot. He gave her the biggest, reddest rose. 595

"Thanks a lot, Art," she said. "See you later." She walked 606
from the room. 609

Then Tim came up. He stuck his finger in his mouth and 621
said, "Say there, you big fellow. Can I have one of those roses, 634
too? How about it, Big Boy?" He winked at Art. 644

[1]

1

raising   blush   starting   couldn't

baseball   night   greenhouse

team   tallest   corner   sailed   coach

2

A	B	C	D
not	rip	at	hide
note	ripe	ate	hid

3

guy   attention   popular   head   friend

pitcher   motorcycle   catcher   idea

4

staring   laughing   doesn't   smiled

Jackson   trying   isn't   throw

players   lesson   crowd   wave

Mark   couldn't   football

ready   shook   walk   sorry

5

The Baseball Lot

Art was having a bad time in school. The kids didn't talk   12
with him, and he didn't know what to say to them. After   24
school, Art would go to the pond to skip stones. And as he   37
skipped them, he said the things he would like to say to Patty.   50

"Patty," he said to himself one day, "I want you to be my girl   64
friend." He skipped a stone and looked at it as it sailed almost   77
to the other side of the pond. Then he said, "No, I <u>will</u> never   91
say anything like that to Patty. I would just blush, and I   103
wouldn't be able to say anything."   109

        [1]

After school one day, Art saw Patty standing on the corner   120
near school. He walked up to her. "Hi, Art," she said.   131

"Hi," he said. He breathed in deeply and said, "Can I walk   143
with you?"   145

She smiled and said, "I'm waiting for somebody, Art. Sorry."   155

"That's okay," Art said, and he began to walk down the   166
street. He looked back from time to time. When he was about a   179
block away, he saw Mark Jackson walk up to Patty and begin   191
to walk with her.   195

The next day, one of the kids told him that Mark Jackson   207
was Patty's boy friend. Mark was one of the most popular boys   219
in school and also one of the smartest.   227

        [1]

Later that day, Art went to the pond and skipped stones.   238
The pond was starting to freeze, and the air was cold.   249

"I wish I were a big football player," Art said to himself. He   262
tossed a stone as far as he could. It went all the way to the   277
other side of the pond. Art smiled. He had never skipped a   289
stone that far before.   293

Then winter came. The winter seemed very long to Art.   303

But at last spring came and the trees started to bud. Now it   316
seemed that the kids paid even less attention to Art.   326

        [1]

"Maybe everybody has other things to think about now,"   335
Art said to himself. And they did. Some of them had   346
motorcycles. Some had bikes. Some had boats. Some had girl   356
friends. And some went out for baseball.   363

The baseball team worked out on a lot near the school. Art   375
passed the lot every day. Sometimes he looked at the team   386
before he went to the pond to skip stones or to the greenhouse   399
to help his dad with the roses.   406

One day, Art stopped on his way home. He was standing   417
next to a boy named Bart. "Hi, Art," Bart said. "Take a look at   431
this pitcher they've got. He can make that ball buzz." So Art   443
took a look.   446

[2]

The pitcher seemed to wave his arm around. Then he tossed   457
the ball, and the catcher grabbed it. "Did you see that?" Bart   469
said. "That ball went like a shot."   476

Art smiled. "Was he trying to make the ball go fast?" Art   488
asked.   489

Bart stared at Art. "What do you mean, trying? He made   500
that ball go so fast, it went like a shot."   510

Art shook his head. "That wasn't very fast at all," he said.   522

Bart folded his arms. "Can you throw it any faster?"   532

"Well, yes, I can. I can throw it a lot faster."   543

"That's a good one," Bart said, and started to laugh.   553

[1]

Then Bart called, "Hey, guys, we've got somebody who can   563
throw the ball a lot faster than your pitcher. This guy can do it.   577
He told me so."   581

A lot of other kids began to laugh. Then one of them yelled, 594
"Hey, Coach! Why don't you let Art here show you how to 606
throw the ball?" 609

Art looked at Bart. "Well, I can throw it faster than that," 621
Art said. 623

"Okay, he's ready," Bart yelled. "He just told me so." 633

Everybody was laughing. Art didn't know what to say. He 643
turned around and started to leave. But everybody was yelling, 653
"Come on, Art. The coach wants you to give his boys a lesson. 666
Come on." 668

[2]

1

leaned   catcher   mound   star

heaved   coach   outfit   whip

formed   could   stained

2

A	B	C	D
mope	slim	hate	rode
mop	slime	hat	rod

3

few   forward   shaking   pitcher

asked   thinner   longer   head   just

blowing   moment   silent   we're

tomorrow   attention   hollered   crowd

friend   tossed   popular   stuffed

4

Art's Fast Ball

Art didn't know what to do. He wanted to leave, but   11
everybody was yelling, "Come on, Art, show us how to pitch."   22

Some boys grabbed Art and started to lead him to the   33
pitcher's mound. "Here he is, Coach," one of the boys hollered.   44
"The star pitcher."   47

The coach walked up to Art. He said, "I don't know what 59
this is all about, but we've got work to do out here. So throw 73
the ball to the catcher. That will shut those guys up. Then get 86
out of here." 89

"Okay," Art said. The coach handed him the ball. 98

[1]

Art turned to the coach and said, "Do I just try to throw it 112
at the catcher as hard as I can?" 120

"That's right," the coach said. "Just throw it and get out of 132
here." 133

The ball felt a little too big in Art's hand. It didn't seem to fit 148
as well as a skipping stone. He rubbed it a few times and got a 163
good grip on it. Then he leaned back. 171

"Show them how—if you can," the boys yelled. 180

Art's long arm went back like a whip. Then it came forward 192
like a whip. "Zip—pow." The catcher was on his seat. 203

[1]

Everybody was silent for a moment. Everything was still. 212
Then somebody yelled, "Did you see that?" 219

"No," somebody else yelled. "Did he throw the ball yet?" 229

The catcher was blowing on his hand. He yelled, "Yes, I'll 240
say he did!" 243

Then everybody began to say things like, "Wow!" They 252
didn't yell the way they had before Art had pitched. They just 264
looked at Art and said, "Wow!" 270

The coach said, "Let's see you do that again." 279

The catcher tossed the ball to Art. Everybody fell silent as 290
Art leaned back. His arm went back like a whip. Then he 302

heaved the ball. "Zip—pow." The catcher was on his seat   313
again, shaking his hand and blowing into his mitt.   322

[2]

The coach said, "Wow! I don't think I've ever seen anybody   333
throw a ball that hard."   338

Art said, "I have to go now." He started to walk from the   351
pitcher's mound.   353

The coach said, "Art, I would like you to come out for   365
baseball."   366

Art stopped. "You mean you want me to be on the baseball   378
team?" he said.   381

"Yes," the coach said. "You have a real gift. You can become   393
a fine pitcher."   396

Art wanted to yell, "Hot dog!" But he didn't. He nodded to   408
the coach and said, "Okay, I'll come out tomorrow after   418
school."   419

[1]

When Art reached the crowd on the side lines, everybody   429
stepped back and made a path for him. Bart said, "Good   440
job, Art."   442

Some of the other kids patted Art on the back. "Good   453
pitching," they said.   456

But Art didn't sleep well that night. He kept thinking of   467
pitching. He kept thinking about the way everybody had said,   477
"Good job. Good pitching." He liked the way they said that.   488
He liked the idea of being a star pitcher. The next day after   501
school, he dressed in a baseball outfit.   508

[1]

Art said to one of the other boys on the team, "I've never   521
worn an outfit like this before. It feels sort of funny." And it   534
looked sort of funny. It seemed to make Art look taller than   546
ever. It seemed to make his arms look longer and thinner.   557

The coach met Art near the pitcher's mound. The coach said,   568
"Today I want to see everything you can do with a ball. When I   582
see what you can't do, I'll know what we have to work on."   595

The catcher stuffed a big rag into his catcher's mitt so that   607
Art's fast ball would not sting his hand so much.   617

[2]

Lesson 6

1

which   leaned   couch   chest   high

right   heaved   cheered   mound

coach   should   beaten   jeered

2

curve   nobody   throw   clapped   went

want   friend   head   catch   state

different   pitches   plate   glared

crowd   mistake   fans   batter   stuffed

showed   moment   few   whipped   skinny

3

The School Team

The coach wanted Art to show him everything he could do
with a baseball. The catcher had stuffed a rag into his mitt so
that Art's fast ball would not sting his hand so much.

"Let's see your fast ball," the coach said.

Art leaned back and—"Zip—pow." The catcher said, "Ow!
That rag doesn't help very much." He tossed the ball back to
Art.

Art dropped the ball. He picked it up and looked at the
coach. The coach said, "Now can you make the ball curve?"

"What do you mean?" Art asked.

"Make the ball bend to the left or bend to the right."

"Oh, that," Art said. "Which way do you want me to make it
bend?"

11
24
35
43
53
65
66
78
89
95
107
120
121

The coach stared at Art for a moment. Then he said, "Make   133
it curve to the left."   138

"Okay," Art said.   141

[2]

Art leaned back and to the side. He said to himself, "This is   154
just like making a stone curve to the left."   163

Art's arm whipped out to the side, and the ball went flying.   175
It was going far to the right of the catcher. The catcher began   188
to reach to the right. Then the ball curved and hit him in the   202
chest.   203

"Wow!" the coach said. "Who showed you how to do that?"   214

Art said, "Nobody." Then he told the coach about skipping   224
stones on the pond every day.   230

[1]

The coach had Art throw a lot of balls that day. The coach   243
had him throw balls that curved to the left and balls that   255
curved to the right. The coach had him throw balls that dipped   267
down just before they reached the catcher. He had Art throw   278
balls that jumped up just before they reached the catcher.   288

The crowd on the side lines clapped after every ball Art   299
heaved. And after every ten balls, the coach had a different   310
catcher work with Art. After catching ten of his pitches, a   321
catcher's hand was very sore.   326

[1]

Art worked out with the baseball team for three weeks. Then   337
the team had its first game. The game was with a big school,   350
West High School. West High was always a top team in the   362
state. It had been the best team in the state three years before.   375
Last year, it had been the third-best team in the state. Art's   387
school had never beaten West High in a baseball game.   397

Art didn't sleep well before the game with West High. He 408
kept thinking about the game. He wanted to do a good job. He 421
hoped that he wouldn't throw a bad ball or make a mistake. 433

About two hundred kids from Art's school went to the game. 444
About four hundred kids from West High came to cheer for 455
West. They cheered and cheered. But they jeered as Art's team 466
came out to start the game. 472

[2]

Art didn't like to hear the West High fans jeer at his team. 485
He said to himself, "Why are they yelling those things? They've 496
never seen us play." But the fans from West High kept on 508
jeering and jeering. 511

West High was to bat first. So Art went to the pitcher's 523
mound. The catcher tossed the ball to him, and Art dropped it. 535

"Ha, ha," a fan yelled. "He can't even catch the ball. Get a 548
rake! Can you rake that ball in? Ho, ho." 557

The first batter was a big boy. He held the bat back and 570
glared at Art. Art didn't like the way he glared, and Art tried 583
not to look at the batter. 589

[1]

Art tried to think about pitching. He said to himself, "Don't 600
throw the ball too high. Don't throw it too low. Don't throw it 613
to the left of the plate. Don't throw it to the right of the plate." 628

Art was not thinking well. He was telling himself what he 639
should not do. He should have been telling himself what he 650
should do. He should have been saying, "Throw that ball right 661
over the plate—right over it." 667

Art leaned back and gave the ball a heave. It went about 679
nine feet over the catcher's mitt. 685

[1]

1

wouldn't   reached   coach

breathed   started   streak   called

2

umpire   cheering   catch   silent

fans   who   shouldn't   mumbled

3

sting   string   Chuck   stared

zing   guy   plate   want

weren't   doesn't   isn't   thrown

clapping   shaking   strike   ready

taken   state   moment   pitcher   curve

4

Some Bad Pitches

Art had just thrown a bad ball. And the West High fans   12
were cheering and clapping. "That's the way to pitch," they   22
yelled.   23

The catcher tossed the ball back to Art, and Art dropped it.   35
The West High fans cheered again. The fans from Art's school   46
were silent.   48

Art picked up the ball. He breathed in and out three times.   60
Then he said to himself, "Don't throw the ball too high. Don't   72
throw the ball too high." Art was not thinking well again.   83

Art heaved the ball. It went like a streak. But it went about   96
ten feet over the catcher's head. The catcher called time out   107
and ran to the pitcher's mound.   113

[1]

The fans from West High cheered. "Get another pitcher," 122
they yelled. "This one has had it." 129

The catcher said, "What's the matter, Art?" 136

"I don't know," Art said. His hand was shaking. "I can't 147
make the ball go where I want it to go." 157

"Yes, you can, Art," the catcher said. "Just think about 167
skipping stones. I'll hold out my mitt. You must throw that 178
ball right into the mitt. Throw it just like you throw a stone. 191
You can do it." 195

"I'll try," Art said. 199

The catcher jogged back, and Art rubbed the ball around in 210
his hand. He looked at the catcher's mitt, and he said to 222
himself, "I'll throw that ball right into the mitt. I'll do it." 234

[1]

Now Art was thinking the right way. He leaned back. His 245
arm whipped back. The ball came from his hand like a shot. 257
"Zip—pow." 259

"Strike one," called the umpire. 264

The fans from Art's school cheered. The fans from West 274
High mumbled. They said, "Was that a lucky toss?" 283

Art got ready for his next pitch. Everybody was silent. 293
"Zip—pow." The catcher was down. 299

"Strike two," the umpire called. 304

The batter did not have a mean look now. He got set for the 318
next pitch. He hadn't taken a swing at any of Art's pitches so 331
far. Now he seemed set to take a swing at the next ball. 344

[1]

Art leaned back and—"Zip—pow." The catcher was down. 354
And the batter began to swing after the ball had reached the 366
catcher. 367

The fans from Art's school cheered and cheered. They 376
jumped up and down. They hugged each other. They yelled, 386
"Go to it, Art. Show them how to pitch." 395

The fans from West were very silent. Then some of them 406
began to cheer, "Come on, Chuck. Get a hit off that pitcher." 418

Chuck was the next batter. He smiled as he walked up to the 431
plate. The catcher jogged out to talk to Art. "This guy is 443
good," the catcher said. "He is one of the best batters in the 456
state. Don't give him anything he can hit." 464

[2]

So Art began to think to himself, "Don't give him anything 475
he can hit. Don't give him a slow ball." 484

Art was not thinking right again. He was thinking about 494
what he shouldn't do. He should have been thinking about 504
what he should do. He was telling himself, "Don't throw a slow 516
ball." 517

And what do you think Art did? He gave Chuck the biggest 529
slow ball you have ever seen. And Chuck hit that ball right out 542
of the park. The fans from West High jumped up and down. 554
They hugged each other. They cheered and yelled. "A home 564
run! A home run!" 568

[1]

The catcher jogged out to talk with Art again. The catcher 579
said, "Art, that was a bad pitch. You can throw better than 591
that. Just zing the ball in. Just think about skipping stones. 602
You can do it." 606

The next batter came up. He was as tall as Art. The fans 619
clapped and cheered when he got near the plate. "You are the 631
best, Bob," one of them yelled. 637

Art remembered that Bob was the best batter on the West 648
team. For a moment, Art began to think about the things that 660
he should not do. Then he remembered what the catcher had 671
said. He stared at the catcher's mitt, and he said to himself, 683
"I'll just zing the ball right into that mitt." 692

[2]

1

started always whistle also

groaned almost reared wound

2

league since pitcher couldn't two

different what went want

3

batters crowded handshakes struck

done tried tired there's stared

star care Tigers you'll doesn't

hadn't weren't winner ducked

4

Art Becomes a Star

The best batter on the West team was at the plate. Art was   13
thinking about what the catcher had told him. Art reared   23
back. He let the ball fly. "Zip—pow." The catcher was on his   36
seat again.   38

"Strike one," the umpire called.   43

"You can do it, Bob," the West fans yelled.   52

Art got the ball again. He looked at the catcher's mitt. He   64
reared back and let the ball fly. The ball started to go right at   78
the batter. The batter ducked down. But almost before he could   89
move, the ball curved and went right into the catcher's mitt.   100

"Strike two," the umpire called.   105

[1]

Again Art wound up and let the ball fly. Bob took a big 118
swing at it, but the ball was in the catcher's mitt before Bob 131
began to swing. 134

"Strike three. You're out." 138

"Oh, no," the West High School fans groaned. 146

"Go, Art, go," the fans from Art's school yelled. 155

And Art went. He struck out every other batter in the game. 167
Art did not do well when he tried to bat, but his team was the 182
winner. They beat West High School 3 to 1. 191

Everybody from Art's school yelled and crowded around 199
Art. They cheered. They patted him on the back. They gave 210
him handshakes and smiles. 214

[1]

Art was so happy that he just sat down after all of the fans 228
had left. He just sat and remembered the game. "Wow!" he said 240
to himself. "I did it." 245

After that first game, things were different in school. The 255
kids smiled at Art. They went out of their way to talk to him. 269
Art felt a lot better about school. In fact, school was a lot of 283
fun for Art now. He waved to the girls. He wasn't afraid to talk 297
to girls. He didn't look down when he talked to them. He had 310
done that before, but now he was Art the Star, the big pitcher. 323

[1]

And Art started to talk like a star. He began to act like a big 338
star. He began to make fun of some of the other kids. He began 352
to show off in front of the girls. He began to talk a lot more. 367

One day, he said to himself, "I want Patty to be my girl 380
friend." So he walked up to her before class and said, "I'm not 393
doing anything after school, so why don't we go for a walk?" 405

"No, thanks, Art," she said. 410

Art didn't know what to say then. Since he had become a 422
pitching star, nobody said, "No, thanks, Art." They always 431
said, "Yes, Art." 434

[2]

Art looked at Patty. "If that's the way you want it," he said, 447
and walked down the hall. He started to whistle, just to show 459
her that he didn't care if she went with him. But he felt bad. He 474
liked Patty. But there was something in the way she talked that 486
told Art, "I don't like you, Art." 493

Art was still thinking about Patty when somebody said, 502
"Art. Art. The coach wants to see you right now." 512

"What does he want?" Art said. 518

The boy said, "I don't know, but it's something big." 528

[1]

Art went with the boy to see the coach. The coach said, 540
"Art, there's going to be a big league baseball game in town. 552
And before the game, they want some of the best high school 564
pitchers to throw for the batters. I want you to throw for our 577
school." 578

"Will I play in the game?" Art said. 586

"No," the coach said. "The Reds will be playing the Tigers. 597
But before the game, you will pitch to some of the batters. 609
Some of the other high schools are sending pitchers to do the 621
same thing." 623

"That will be fun," Art said. 629

His coach said, "You'll be pitching to some of the best 640
batters in baseball." 643

[2]

1

reared falling m<u>ou</u>nd <u>a</u>lso w<u>a</u>ited

<u>A</u>rt f<u>ir</u>st spe<u>a</u>ker <u>Ga</u>rner h<u>ar</u>dest

l<u>ea</u>gue sh<u>ou</u>ldn't <u>a</u>lmost <u>a</u>lways

2

<u>worry</u> <u>voice</u> <u>exhibition</u> stands

jogged filed Hunt blinked

shaking umpire James o'clock

started stared struck

3

First Inning

Art was going to pitch to some big league players before the 　　12
game on Sunday. His coach had told him that he would be 　　24
pitching to some of the best batters in baseball. 　　33

The game was to start at one o'clock. Art was to begin 　　45
pitching at noon. But at 12 o'clock there were not very many 　　57
fans in the stands. Art walked to the pitcher's mound and 　　68
picked up the ball. One of the players from the Tigers said, 　　80
"Just throw fast balls. The batter will hit them <u>into</u> the left 　　92
stands. Some of the fans will get free baseballs." 　　101

[1]

Art looked up at the left stands. About one hundred kids 　　112
were up there. Some of them had baseball mitts. Art said, 　　123
"Should I throw as hard as I can?" 　　131

"That's right," the player said. "Don't worry, the batter will 　　141
hit the ball. You're pitching to James Hunt. He'll hit them, all 　　153
right." 　　154

Art stared at the catcher's mitt. Then Art reared back and   165
gave the ball the hardest heave he could give it. "Zip—pow."   177
The catcher was on his seat.   183

The player who was standing next to Art blinked and stared   194
at Art. James Hunt looked at the catcher, and then he looked   206
at Art. He blinked.   210

[1]

A fan yelled, "Did you see that? He shot that ball past James   223
Hunt."   224

Another fan said, "Hunt is trying to make the kid look good.   236
He'll belt the next ball."   241

But Hunt didn't have time to swing at the next ball. Before   253
he began his swing, the catcher was on his seat again.   264

The catcher jogged out to the pitcher's mound. He said,   274
"Hey, kid, how do you do that? No pitcher has ever set me on   288
my seat before. How do you do that?"   296

"I just throw hard," Art said.   302

And he did throw hard. He struck out James Hunt.   312

[1]

Art struck out other batters that day. Not many fans were in   324
the park to see what Art had done, but every fan who was there   338
was standing and clapping when Art left the pitcher's mound.   348

Art walked over to his coach and sat down. His coach had   360
tears in his eyes. "You are the best," his coach said.   371

Then the coach for the Tigers walked up and sat down next   383
to Art. He said, "Not many fans saw that. How would you like   396
to pitch the first inning of the game? I think the fans should see   410
what you can do. If you can strike out my Tigers the way you   424

did, I'll bet you can strike out any player on the Reds." 436

"Okay," Art said, and he smiled. 442

[2]

Art was thinking, "Wow! I get to pitch to big league batters 454
in a big league game." 459

The fans filed into the ball park, and Art waited. Then a 471
voice came over the loud speaker. It said, "Today a boy from 483
your town will pitch for the Tigers in the first inning. This boy 496
is one of the best pitchers we have seen. His name is Art 509
Garner." 510

The fans who had seen Art pitch before the game cheered 521
and clapped. But the other fans didn't cheer. 529

[1]

One of the fans said, "We didn't come here to see kids play. 542
We came to see the Reds and the Tigers." 551

Art walked to the mound. Then he looked up at the stands. 563
He had never seen so many fans before. Suddenly he became 574
afraid. He began to think about all of the things that he 586
shouldn't do. "Don't throw the ball too high," he told himself. 597

The catcher tossed the ball to Art. And Art dropped it. 608

"Boooooo," yelled some of the fans. "Get that bum out of 619
here." Art's hands felt cold, and his legs were shaking. 629

[2]

1

thousand   leaving   roared

waited   cheered   first   while

these   crash   leaned   right

proud   reared   afraid   sharp

2

records   nurse   put   watched

turn   voice   shy   awake   worry

brakes   catcher's   dollars   hospital

mixed   driver   closer   strapped

showed   lonely   onto   two   alive

exhibition   fist   shake   cast

woman   booing   foot   open   people

3

Things Take a Bad Turn

    Art was standing on the pitcher's mound. His hands felt   10
cold. The fans were yelling and booing because he had dropped   21
the ball. The catcher yelled to him, "Come on, Art. Just zip it   34
right in here." He pounded his fist into his mitt.   44

    Art stared at that mitt. He stared and stared. "Look at that   56
mitt," he told himself. Now he was thinking the right way   67
again. He said, "I'm going to zip that ball right into the mitt."   80
He leaned back and shot the ball at the catcher's mitt. The   92
batter didn't have time to start his <u>swing</u>. The catcher was on   104
his seat.   106

"Strike one," the umpire called.   111

[2]

The fans began to say, "Did you see that?" Then the fans fell   124
silent as Art reared back for his next pitch. "Zip—pow." Down   136
went the catcher again.   140

"Strike two."   142

"Wow!" the fans yelled. Then they waited for Art's next   152
pitch.   153

Again Art heaved the ball so hard that the batter did not   165
have time to swing. "Strike three. You're out."   173

The fans clapped and cheered.   178

Art struck out the next batter with three pitches.   187

[1]

The last batter took a swing at Art's fast ball, but he missed   200
it by a foot. As Art walked from the pitcher's mound, all of the   214
fans were standing and clapping. The players from the Tigers   224
and the Reds came out to shake hands with him.   234

Art felt proud. "Just think," he said to himself. "Last year, I   246
was lonely and shy. But look at me now. I'm a star."   258

And he was a star. That night his dad showed him the paper.   271
There was a story about Art and his pitching. "I'm proud of   283
you, Art," his dad said.   288

[1]

People from the big league came over to talk to Art that   300
night. A man from the Reds said that he would pay Art three   313
hundred thousand dollars if Art left school and became a   323
pitcher for the Reds. A woman from the Tigers told Art that   335
she would give Art five hundred thousand dollars if Art played   346
with the Tigers.   349

Art told them that he would have to think about leaving 360
school. 361

Then some of Art's friends came over. They wanted to take 372
Art to a party. Art asked his dad and mom, and they said that 386
it was all right for him to go. 394

[1]

So Art got in the car. The driver zipped down the road from 407
Art's farm. He went faster and faster. "This car is very fast," he 420
told Art. Art did not like to go fast, but Art didn't want the 434
other kids to think that he was afraid. So he didn't say 446
anything. 447

The car roared down the road. Just then a truck turned onto 459
the road. The driver hit the brakes. The car began to slide. It 472
slid to the left, and then it went back to the right. 484

Nobody said a thing. They just watched the car come closer 495
and closer to the truck. Closer. Closer. 502

[1]

When Art opened his eyes, he was looking at a green wall. 514
He started to move. Then he saw that he was strapped into a 527
bed. He felt a sharp pain in his arm. His arm was in a cast. 542

He looked around the room. A nurse was reading Art's 552
records. When she saw that Art was awake, she put down his 564
records and said, "Well, did you have a good sleep?" 574

"Where am I?" Art asked. 579

"You're in the hospital," the nurse said. "You are lucky to be 591
alive." 592

"What happened?" Art said. Everything seemed mixed up. 600

"You were in a bad crash," she said. "A very bad crash." 612

[2]

Lesson 11

1

n<u>ea</u>rly   sh<u>ou</u>ld   <u>outside</u>

l<u>ea</u>gue   rememb<u>er</u>

2

<u>curl</u>   <u>stairs</u>   watched   scratched

itched   awake   sawed   broken

hospital   strapped   crying   alone

begun   drove   few   believe

3

two   there's   chair   nurse

rubbed   cast   passed   records

else   wanted   tried   somewhere

4

He'll Never Pitch Again

Art was in the hospital. The nurse had just told him that he   13
had been in a very bad crash. Art didn't remember the crash.   25
He had a hard time thinking. His arm was in pain.   36

A doctor came into the room. The nurse said, "He's awake   47
now."   48

The doctor walked up to Art's bed. "How do you feel?" she   60
asked.   61

"I don't know," Art said. It was hard to think. "There's a   73
pain in my right arm. Why is it in a cast?"   84

"Your arm is broken," the doctor said.   91

"That's the arm I throw with," Art said. "<u>I</u>s it bad? Will I be   105
able to pitch soon?"   109

[1]

The doctor looked down. Then she stood up. "We should   119
talk about this later," she said. "Right now, you should get   130
some sleep."   132

"Tell me," Art said. "Will my arm be okay?"   141

The doctor rubbed her chin. "I'm afraid not," she said.   151
"Your arm was broken in three spots. I don't think you'll ever   163
be able to pitch again."   168

"No," Art said. "No, no." He began to sob. Art wanted to   180
curl up into a little ball and hide. He wanted to be somewhere   193
else. He wanted to believe that he was having a bad dream.   205

[1]

But Art's arm was in pain, and he kept hearing the words the   218
doctor had said. "I don't think you'll ever be able to pitch   230
again."   231

The doctor sat next to him on the bed. "I know that I can't   245
say anything that will help," the doctor said. "But you must be   257
brave. You feel as if your life is over, but it has just begun. I   272
know."   273

Art looked up at the doctor. The doctor seemed to float in   285
the tears that were coming from Art's eyes. He turned from the   297
doctor.   298

[1]

Art had been in the hospital for nearly two weeks. A lot of   311
kids had come to visit him, but he didn't see any of them. He   325
told the doctor that he didn't want to see anybody but his mom   338
and dad.   340

Patty came to the hospital one day, but Art didn't see her. He   353
didn't want her to see him with his broken arm. He didn't want   366
her to see him when he was in bed—all strapped up like a   380

baby. Two of the other kids who were in the car with Art were 394
in the hospital, but Art didn't want to see them. 404

On the day Art was to leave the hospital, the nurse asked if 417
he would stop in and see his friends. "No," he said. "I want to 431
go home." He wanted to be home. He wanted to be alone. 443

[1]

So he went home. His mom and dad came to the hospital to 456
get him. His mom had been crying. His dad tried to be happy 469
and tell jokes. But Art didn't say much. He sat in the car and 483
watched the road as his dad drove home. 491

Art didn't go to school the next week. He sat. He didn't eat 504
much or sleep much. He just sat. He sat on the stairs. He sat in 519
a chair. He even went down and sat near the pond for a while. 533
But that made him sad. He felt like skipping stones across the 545
pond, but then he remembered that he would never throw well 556
again. So he went back to the stairs and sat. 566

His arm was still in a cast, and it itched. But he couldn't 579
scratch it. He tried to slap it, but it still itched. He scratched 592
the outside of the cast, but that didn't help. He wanted to get 605
rid of that cast. 609

[2]

Art wanted to go away from his home and his school. But he 622
didn't know where to go. Two more weeks passed. Then it was 634
time for the cast to come off. Art sat in the doctor's office and 648
watched the doctor saw the cast. As the doctor sawed, Art said 660
to himself, "I hope she doesn't saw my arm." 669

The cast came off in two parts. Art's arm felt funny. And it 682
looked funny. It was thin. Art tried to bend it. It didn't bend. 695
He tried again. It bent an inch or two. 704

The doctor said, "Take it easy. We'll start giving that arm 715
some work in a few days, but don't try to bend it too much." 729

Art looked at his arm and said to himself, "So that's the arm 742
that struck out three Reds in one inning. I can't even bend the 755
arm." 756

[2]

1

di<u>r</u>t   ar<u>ou</u>nd   <u>sh</u>ame   w<u>ea</u>k

<u>t</u>old   <u>f</u>i<u>r</u>st   r<u>ai</u>sed

<u>h</u>ardly   <u>a</u>lways   ab<u>ou</u>t

2

<u>heavy</u>   <u>exercise</u>   friends   tried

skip   everybody   walked   front

month   care   believe   stared   fair

sorry   moped   nodded   across

again   lonely   watched   stairs   fifty

3

Art Feels Sorry for Himself

The cast had been taken from Art's arm. And Art went back   12
to school for the first time. Everybody tried to be friends. At   24
least fifty kids told Art that they were sorry. But Art didn't say   37
much. He just nodded and walked away. He went to his botany   49
class and sat down.   53

Patty was sitting in front of him. She turned around and held   65
up a big red rose. "Here's one that I raised," she said. "What do   79
you think of it?"   83

Art said, "It's pretty. It's very pretty."   90

She smiled and turned back. Art didn't like the <u>way</u> she   101
acted. Why didn't she say, "I'm sorry, Art"?   109

[1]

Patty didn't even seem to care. Art would never pitch again,   120
and she didn't even care. After class, he walked up to her in the   134
hall. He didn't know what he would say to her, but he wanted   147

to talk. He wanted to hear her say that she was sorry. Art said, 161
"I had my cast taken off." 167

"I see that," she said. 172

Art said, "The doctor said that I'll never pitch again." 182

She stared at him. Then she asked, "Do you believe that?" 193

"Yes," Art said. "She's a doctor. She should know." 202

Patty said, "Do you want to believe that you'll never pitch 213
again?" 214

Art said, "No. I want to pitch." 221

[1]

Patty said, "Tell yourself that you can pitch, and you will 232
pitch." 233

"No," Art said. "I don't think so. I can hardly bend my 245
arm." 246

Patty said, "Maybe you don't want to bend your arm. Maybe 257
you want to feel sorry for yourself." 264

Art felt his cheeks getting red. "I don't feel sorry for myself," 276
he said, and walked away from her. 283

But Art did feel sorry for himself. He kept thinking about 294
what a shame it was that he would never pitch again. He kept 307
thinking about what a shame it was that his arm had been 319
broken. And he liked to hear people say, "I'm sorry, Art." It 331
was a lot better than being lonely. 338

[2]

Art didn't talk to Patty for a month. He moped around 349
school, and he moped around the farm. He went to the doctor's 361
office three times a week. The doctor had him do exercises for 373
his arm. Now Art could bend his arm almost all the way. But 386
his arm was weak. It was so weak that he couldn't bend it when 400
he held a heavy steel ball. The doctor told him that he should 413

exercise his arm at home every day, but Art didn't feel like 425

exercising. So his arm didn't get very strong. 433

[1]

    A year passed, and his arm was still not strong. Some of the 446
kids in school still talked about how good Art had been at 458
pitching, but they didn't talk about him very much. And he 469
didn't talk to them very much. He went to class and worked 481
pretty hard, but not too hard. He helped his dad, and he did a 495
fair job, but not a good job. And he still felt sorry for himself. 509

    Then one day something happened. He was walking near the 519
pond when he saw Patty riding a horse on the dirt road that 532
went past the pond. 536

[1]

    "Hi, Art," Patty called. She rode her horse next to him, 547
stopped, and slid down from the horse. 554

    She said, "What are you doing, skipping stones?" 562

    "No," Art said. "I don't skip stones any more." 571

    "Why not?" she asked. 575

    "My arm," Art said. He felt himself getting mad. "I can't 586
throw any more." 589

    "Let's see you try," she said. 595

    "No," he said. "I can't do it. At one time, I could skip a stone 610
all the way across the pond. But that was when I had a good arm." 625

    "Let's see how you do now," she said. 633

    "No," Art said. "And I don't want to talk about it any more." 646

[2]

Lesson 13

1   sh<u>o</u>re   th<u>ir</u>d   h<u>ea</u>ved   sque<u>e</u>ze   f<u>ar</u>ther

2   <u>once</u>   <u>challenges</u>   plunk

wing   brave   flies

ashamed   fifth   exercise

3   skim   heavy   since   stiff   side   sunk

flat   another   being   across   along   stone

heavy   throwing   month   you'll   pressed

4

Patty Challenges Art

Patty was making Art mad. She was trying to get him to 12
skip stones, but he didn't want to. He felt ashamed of himself. 24

Patty picked up a stone and smiled at him. She said, "If 36
you're so bad at skipping stones, I'll bet I could beat you in a 50
contest." She looked out over the pond. She pressed her lips. 61
Then she tossed the stone. "Plunk," it went, and it sank. It 73
didn't skip one time. 77

Art smiled. He said, "That was pretty bad." 85

She said, "I'll do better with this next stone." She picked up 97
the stone, <u>pressed</u> her lips, and gave it a big toss. "Plunk." 109
[1]

Art laughed. Then he said, "You're not throwing the right 119
way. You've got to get your arm down low so that you can skim 133
the stone across the water." 138

She picked up another stone and held her arm to her side. 150
"Like this?" she asked. 154

"Sort of," Art said. 158

She made a face and tossed the stone. It skipped once. 169
"There," she said. "Let's see you beat that." 177

Art laughed. "That wouldn't be very hard to beat." He 187
picked up a stone. He leaned to the side. His arm felt stiff and 201
funny when he went to whip it back. He tried to swing fast, but 215
his arm seemed to move very slowly. 222

[1]

The stone skipped three times. It went farther than Patty's 232
stone. But the stone went less than a third of the way across 245
the pond. Art was thinking to himself, "At one time I could 257
skip a stone all the way across the pond." 266

Patty said, "That wasn't bad, but I'll bet I can beat it." She 279
picked up a flat stone, bent to the side, and let it fly. It went 294
almost as far as Art's stone. 300

Art picked up a stone. "I'll make this one zip," he said. He 313
bent to the side and let it fly. It went over a third of the way 329
across the pond. 332

[1]

"That was good," Patty said. "Do you still think that you'll 343
never pitch again?" 346

Art sat down on the shore of the pond. He didn't say 358
anything for some time. Then he said, "At one time, I could 370
skip a stone to the other side of the pond. Now I can't skip it 385
anywhere near the other side." 390

Patty said, "But this is the first time you've thrown since you 402
broke your arm. I'll bet you that within a month you'll be 414
throwing a lot better. But you'll have to work at it every day." 427

[1]

Art said, "I once read that a bird with a broken wing never   440
flies as high again."   444

Patty said, "Stop that. You're not a bird. And you don't have   456
a broken wing. They fixed your arm. You just have to start   468
being brave."   470

Art glared at her. "What do you mean? What makes you   481
think I'm not brave?"   485

She grabbed his hand and gave it a squeeze. Then she said,   497
"You don't like being you. You like being a pitcher. You like   509
being a show-off. You like feeling sorry for yourself. But you   520
don't like being Art Garner."   525

"That's not right," Art said. "I like being me."   534

[2]

Patty said, "Then stop being ashamed of yourself. Stop   543
feeling sorry for yourself. Start working with yourself. You can   554
be a pitcher if you want to. Maybe you won't be as good as you   569
were. Maybe you'll have to work very hard. But if you set   581
yourself to do it, you can do it."   589

For the next five days, Art kept thinking about what Patty   600
had said. On the fifth day, he said to himself, "She's right. If I   614
want to be a pitcher, I'm going to tell myself that I can do it.   629
And then I will do it. I'll work until I do it."   641

On the next day, Art began to work. He began to exercise his   654
arm. He began skipping stones on the pond again. At first he   666
didn't try to throw them very hard, but each day he heaved a   679
little harder.   681

[2]

1 **tch**

A	B
catch	pitcher
itch	hatch
match	catcher

2 nearly   brains   hardly

floated   call   heaved

3 glared   slowly   watch   quit   curve

tested   timing   foot   umpire   halfway

tried   cried   signaled   gripped   there's

facts   locker   inning   fly   try   league

throwing   swing   coach   once   player

flashing   smartest   guy   blow

4

The Smartest Pitcher

Art became better, but it seemed very slow to him. After 11
working for two months, Art could hardly throw a stone 21
halfway across the pond. After six months, he could throw a 32
stone a little more than halfway across the pond. After almost 43
a year, he could make a stone skip pretty far—but not nearly as 57
far as he had before he'd broken his arm. 66

Art went out for baseball the next spring. The first time he 78
was on the pitcher's mound, the boys on the team yelled, 89
"Come on, Art. Set that catcher on his seat." 98

[1]

Art heaved the ball just as hard as he could, but the catcher 111
didn't go down. Art didn't have the same fast ball that he had 124
before. The catcher didn't drop his mitt and blow on his hand 136
after catching one of Art's fast balls. 143

Art wanted to quit the team after that first day. But when he 156
was in the locker room, the coach came up to him. The coach 169
sat down next to him and said, "Art, let's look at the facts. You 183
don't have that flashing fast ball that you had before. But you 195
can still become a good pitcher. You can make the ball curve. 207
You can make the ball hop." 213

[1]

The coach said, "Before, you didn't have to make it curve or 225
hop. You could just lay back and throw your fast ball. But now 238
you're going to have to think. Before you broke your arm, you 250
would win games with your arm. Now you're going to have to 262
win games with your brains. Remember that—your brains." 271

In the first game Art's brain was tested. The test came in the 284
first inning. 286

Art struck out the first batter with a fast ball. He started to 299
think, "Maybe my fast ball has come back." So when the next 311
batter stepped up to the plate, Art reared back and let fly with 324
another fast ball. 327

"Crack." The batter hit the ball hard. It was a three-base hit. 339
[2]

Now Art was afraid. A player was on third base. There was 351
one out. And Art didn't have a flashing fast ball that would 363
strike out the other batters. 368

The catcher jogged out and said to Art, "Just make the old 380
brain work, Art. You can strike this next guy out. Just throw 392
the kind of pitch he's not looking for. Watch me. I'll give you 405
some signals." 407

So Art watched the catcher. The catcher signaled for a slow 418
curve. "No," Art said to himself. "He'll hit it out of the park." 431
Then Art began to think, "Maybe he won't. Maybe he's 441
looking for a very fast ball. Maybe a curve will throw his 453
timing off and make him miss the ball." 461
[2]

So Art leaned back. He whipped his arm back just the way 473
he did when he was throwing a fast ball. Then he let the ball 487
go. But he didn't throw it fast. He floated it. The batter swung 500
and missed the ball by a foot. 507

The batter gripped the bat and glared at Art. Art smiled at 519
the catcher. That seemed to make the batter madder than ever. 530
The catcher signaled for a ball outside the plate. Art heaved the 542
ball. 543

The batter started to swing before he saw that the ball was 555
pitched outside. He missed. Now the catcher called for a fast 566
ball. Art heaved it as hard as he could. "Strike three," the 578
umpire called. 580

[1]

Art struck out the next batter. In that game Art struck out 8 593
more batters, and Art's team was the winner. 601

And that's how Art got started years ago. Today he is a big 614
league player. He's not as good as he would have been if he 627
hadn't broken his arm. He's not the best in the league. But he is 641
one of the best. He's happy because he's doing something he 652
likes to do. And he's smart. He may not have the fastest fast 665
ball in the big leagues. But they say he's the smartest pitcher in 678
the game. 680

And there's one more thing. Art's biggest fan is his wife, 691
Patty. 692

[1]

1

A	B	C
ir	girl	first
ur	fern	turn
er	hurt	thirst
	jerk	her

2 **tch**

A	B
match	itch
pitcher	catcher
catch	latch

3 fla<u>sh</u> <u>ch</u>in <u>a</u>lso <u>r</u>i<u>gh</u>t <u>r</u>ea<u>ch</u>ed <u>wa</u>l<u>l</u>et

4 <u>quite</u> escaped president watch pay driver

pockets private fare moment officer

blinked duds instant twenty hotel wig

matter hundred bridal taking talking security

glared guy faking throw bribe woman

couldn't once friend without somewhere

5

A Ride to the Docks

The con man and the president had escaped from the hotel. 11
They were in a cab. The con man had gotten rid of his wig and 26
his bridal dress. He was thinking, "The president is very odd. I 38
must leave and hide somewhere." 43

The president said to the cab driver, "Take us to the docks. 55
We are going to take a trip on a ship because we want to leave 70
this town." 72

So the cab went to the docks. Then the driver said, "That 84
will be six dollars." 88

The president turned to the con man. "Private," he said, 98
"pay the driver." 101

[1]

The con man said, "I don't have any cash. But you have two 114
hundred dollars." 116

The president said, "Yes, yes. So I do." 124

Then he reached into his pockets. "I can't seem to find my 136
cash," he said after a moment. The president was faking. He 147
said, "Stay here. I'll be back in a flash with the cash." 159

The president left the cab and walked up to a woman who 171
looked very rich. The president said, "Where is your pass?" 181

The woman looked at the president and blinked. "What 190
pass? I don't know what you're talking about." 198

The president said, "I'm a security officer. You can't be in 209
this part of the docks unless you have a pass. Show me your 222
pass, or I'll have to lock you up." 230

[2]

"But I don't have a pass," the woman said. "Nobody told me 242
about a pass." 245

"You had better come along with me, then," the president 255
said, and he grabbed the woman by the arm. He began to lead 268
the woman to the cab. 273

The woman said, "Wait a moment, officer. Can't I pay you 284
for a pass? If I were to give you some money, couldn't you take 298
care of the matter for me?" 304

The president asked, "Are you trying to bribe a security 314
officer?" 315

"No, no," the woman said. "I would never think of doing 326
that. I just had the idea that you might be able to get a pass for 342
me." 343

[1]

The president rubbed his chin. Then he said, "All right. Give 354
me twenty dollars, and I'll give you a pass. But you must 366
remember that the pass is just good for today. If I ever see you 380
in this spot again without a pass, I'll throw you in jail." 392

The woman said, "I'll never be here without a pass. I was 404
here to meet a friend who was—" 411

"Just give me the twenty bucks," the president said. 420

"Yes, sir," the woman said. She got her wallet and handed 431
the president twenty dollars. 435

[1]

The president stuck the money in his pocket. Then he took 446
out a pen. "Give me your hand," he said to the woman. 458

The woman held out her hand, and the president made a big 470
X on the back of the woman's hand. "There," the president 481
said. "Just show that X to any cop who tries to stop you." 494

"Oh, thank you very much," the woman said. 502

The president went back to the cab. He asked the driver, 513
"How much was the fare?" 518

"Six dollars," the cab driver said. 524

"Here you are, driver," the president said. He handed the cab 535
driver ten dollars. Then he said, "Keep it all." 544

"Thank you," the driver said. 549

"That's quite all right," the president said. He smiled. 558

[2]

Then the president turned to the con man and said, "Private, 569
do you plan to sit in that cab all day? There is no spot in my 585
army for those who sit around." 591

The con man started to say, "But I was just waiting—" 602

"Hush up," the president said. "Get out of the cab this 613
instant." 614

The con man got out of the cab. He was thinking to himself, 627
"I must find a way to get away from this guy." 638

The president said, "Before we leave on our trip, we must get 650
some fine duds. Who would think of going on a trip without 662
fine duds?" 664

[1]

1

A	B	C
ir	firm	thirst
ur	surf	serve
er	her	fir
	fur	clerk

2

proudly   batch   our   salt

stormed   pitcher   foolish

3

A	B
up	upset
steam	steamship
over	oversight

4

assistant   door   foolish   Japan   papers

Henry   shocked   strokes   fuss   yesterday

bridal   Robert   expected   shop   dashed

Fredrick   mistake   quickly   Reeves

smiled   bribe   stared   doesn't   lies

5

Sir Robert Fredrick

The president and the con man were at the docks. The   11
president had two hundred and ten dollars. He had gotten two   22
hundred dollars from the hotel by telling the clerk in the hotel   34
that there were bugs in the bridal rooms. When he and the con   47
man went to the docks, the president had gotten twenty dollars   58
from a rich woman. He had given ten dollars to the cab driver.   71

Now the president and the con man were walking along the   82
docks. The con man asked, "Where are we going?"   91

The president said, "Will you stop asking foolish <u>questions</u>!   100
We're going on a trip. I need a good rest at sea."   112
                                                                  [2]

"But . . . ," the con man started to say.   119

"Private, if you ever want to become anything but a private,   130
you must remember to take orders. Just do what I tell you to do."   144

The president and the con man went up to a shop. Over the   157
door of the shop were these words: JAPAN STEAMSHIP   166
LINES.   167

The president stormed into the shop. He dashed up to the   178
woman at the desk and said, "Just what kind of a line are you   192
running? They tell me that my bags are not here yet. And your   205
man picked them up yesterday."   210
                                                                  [1]

The woman behind the desk said, "There must be some   220
mistake. If we picked up your bags, they're here."   229

"There is a mistake, all right," the president said. "And you   240
made it. How do you expect my assistant and me to go on this   254

trip without our bags? How do you expect us to do our work in   268
Japan if we don't have our papers?"   275

"I will look into the matter right now," the woman said.   286

"Before you do," the president said, "let me check on another   297
thing. Where is your list of those who are going on this trip?"   310
The woman handed a list to the president.   318

[1]

The president looked at the list, and then he said, "Just as I   331
expected. My name is on the list, but my assistant's name is not   344
on the list. I called you three days back and told you that my   358
assistant was going, but you can look for yourself. His name is   370
not on this list."   374

"What is your assistant's name?" the woman asked.   382

"Reeves. Henry Reeves," the president said.   388

The woman looked at the list. Then she smiled and said,   399
"You must have looked at the list too quickly. His name is   411
here." The woman held up the list and showed the president.   422

[1]

The president looked shocked. He stared at the list of names.   433
Then he said, "I am sorry for making such a fuss. I was so   447
upset about our bags that I must have looked right past the   459
name on the list."   463

The president was telling lies left and right. He had seen the   475
name "Henry Reeves" on the list. In fact, he had looked at the   488
name before he said that his assistant's name was Henry   498
Reeves. The president had just picked a name from the list and   510
had given it to the con man.   517

[1]

The woman behind the desk stared at the president and   527
asked, "And what is your name?"   533

The president blinked. "Sir Robert Fredrick," he said 541
proudly. 542

The woman looked at the list. Then she said, "We have a 554
Robert Fredrick listed here, but the list doesn't show that you 565
are a 'sir.' " 568

The president stared at the woman behind the desk. "Well, 578
my good woman," the president said, "I think that you can fix 590
that oversight with three strokes of your pen." 598

"Yes, sir," the woman said. She took her pen and made three 610
strokes: "S-i-r." 612

The president smiled. "Now if we can find our bags, we will 624
be set for the trip to Japan." 631

"We will find them," the woman said. 638

[2]

1

A	B
were	hurt
blur	person
stern	firm
churn	jerk
bird	turn

2

ca<u>tch</u>   dep<u>a</u>rtment   l<u>oa</u>ded   <u>wh</u>ispered

rep<u>or</u>t   <u>sh</u>ipping   c<u>ou</u>ldn't   <u>r</u>ight

w<u>ai</u>ting   steam   b<u>oar</u>d   <u>our</u>   l<u>ea</u>ve

3

<u>identification</u>   <u>super</u>   <u>office</u>   belonged

fuss   scare   jacket   sorry   fellow

talking   pretend   task   fool

locate   split   assistant

4

A Cartload of Bags

The president and the con man were in the office of the   12
Japan Steamship Lines. The president was telling lies so fast   22
that the con man couldn't keep up with him. The president had   34
looked at the names of those who were going on a ship to   47
Japan. He had picked two names. Then he had told the woman   59
behind the desk that one of the names belonged to the   70
president. Now the woman behind the desk was saying that she   81

would help the president find his bags.   88

   The woman said, "I will make a call to our shipping   99
<u>department</u> and see if we can locate your bags."   108

[1]

   As the woman called the shipping department, the president   117
turned to the con man and whispered, "I don't want to tell   129
them that I am a president. That would scare them. So I'll just   142
pretend that I'm another person."   147

   The steamship woman said, "I'm happy to report that all of   158
your bags are safe in our shipping department."   166

   The president turned to the con man and said, "You fool.   177
You told me that our bags were not in the shipping department.   189
You must try to take more care when I give you a task to do."   204

   The con man didn't say a thing. He just looked at the   216
president. The con man said to himself, "If I am a con man,   229
the president is a super con man."   236

[2]

   The president turned to the woman who worked for the   246
steamship line and told her that he was sorry about making a   258
fuss over the missing bags. He said, "We will go to your   270
shipping department right now and pick up our bags."   279

   The woman said, "Just go up the ramp at the other end of   292
the dock. The ramp leads to the shipping department."   301

   The con man wanted to leave. He said to himself, "I must   313
split. I can't stand this president any longer. I never know what   325
he'll do next."   328

   But the con man didn't leave. He stayed with the president.   339
He walked up the ramp.   344

[1]

A man in a red jacket was standing at the end of the ramp. 358
The president said, "My name is Sir Robert Fredrick. I have 369
come to pick up my bags." 375

"Yes, sir," the man said. He waved to another man who was 387
sitting in the middle of the shipping department. That man 397
stood up and came running to the man in the red jacket. "Get 410
Sir Robert's bags," the man in the red jacket said. 420

The other man dashed off. Soon he came back with a cart 432
loaded with bags. The president nodded. "Yes," he said. "It 442
seems as if they are all here. Take them on board, my good 455
man." 456

[1]

So the man with the cart took them on board. The president 468
said to the con man, "Follow that fellow. I must go get some 481
more money. We can't have much of a trip if we only have two 495
hundred and ten dollars." 499

The con man walked behind the man with the cart, and all 511
the time the con man walked, he kept saying to himself, "Now 523
is the time to leave. There is no telling how long that guy can 537
go on before somebody nabs him." 543

[1]

But just as the con man was ready to split, somebody came 555
up behind him and said, "Just one moment. Those are my 566
bags. Where are you going with them?" 573

The con man turned around. A tall man was staring at him. 585
The con man stared at the tall man. Then the con man started 598
to say something. But he didn't know what to say. He just said, 611
"Well, I, uh, you see. . . . Well, you know, I, uh . . ." 621

The tall man said, "I am waiting for somebody to tell me   633
what you plan to do with my bags."   641

The con man said, "Well, it's like this, you see. I—that is,   654
we—I mean, you . . ."   658

The tall man looked very mad.   664

[2]

1

found irk reached turned why

wouldn't Herb parked hush

loan were first clever match

2

truth impostor actor along none

flowing stammering wonderful

identification officer stuttering

demand wallet whistle blast

partner hollow hollered victim

crook suddenly buddy opened fooled

3

President Washington Tells the Truth

A tall man had found out that the con man was trying to 13
steal his bags. The con man was trying to think of something 25
to say, but the words were not flowing from his mouth. He was 38
stammering and stuttering and saying, "You know—I mean, 47
you see . . ." The tall man was getting very mad. 56

Then suddenly the president came back. He had a cop with 67
him. He said, "There he is, officer. That tall man is the 79
impostor. Go ask him his name, and you'll see." 88

The cop went up to the tall man. "All right, buddy," he said. 101
"What's your name?" 104

"Fredrick. Robert Fredrick," the tall man said. "And this 113
man seems to be stealing my bags." 120

[1]

The cop asked, "Do you have identification to show who you   131
are?"   132

"Yes," the tall man said. He reached in his pocket and   143
grabbed his wallet. As he opened it, the president said, "Just as   155
I told you, officer. That man stole my wallet, and now he's   167
trying to steal our bags."   172

The cop turned to the tall man. "All right, buddy," he said.   184
"Hand over the wallet."   188

"I will not!" the man shouted. "That is my wallet. Do you   200
hear me? My wallet! I don't know what's going on here, but I   213
demand—"   214

"All right, buddy," the cop said. "Come along and pipe down,   225
or I'll have to call the bus that takes you to the rest home."   239
[2]

"But I haven't done anything," the tall man said. "These men   250
are the crooks."   253

The cop grabbed the wallet. Then he said, "One more peep   264
out of you, buddy, and I'm calling the bus for the rest home."   277

"All right," the man said. "I can see that you are part of the   291
plot. You work together to con rich men at the docks."   302

"That did it," the cop said. He took a whistle from his pocket   315
and gave a loud blast. Soon a bus came up the ramp and   328
parked on the dock.   332
[1]

Three big cops came out and ran up to the president and the   345
other men. The tall man said, "Please hear what I have to say. I   359
am a victim of a plot to con me. These men have taken my bags   374
and my wallet. Now they are trying to lock me up in a rest   388
home. How can they get away with such a crime? Can't you   400
stop them? Please stop them. Please."   406

"He is a very good actor," the president said. "If the cops in 419
our wonderful town were not so smart, he would fool them. We 431
are very lucky to have cops who are not fooled by such clever 444
crooks as this tall man." 449

[2]

"That's right," the first cop said. "This guy can't fool us." 460

Two cops grabbed the tall man. They started to lead him to 472
the bus. The man began to yell, "Where are you taking me? 484
What are you going to do with me?" 492

One cop said, "We're taking you to the Happy Hollow Rest 503
Home." 504

The president said, "One moment, officer. Where did you say 514
you were going?" 517

"Happy Hollow," the cop said. 522

The president said, "In that case, I have something to tell 533
you. This man is the real Robert Fredrick. These are his bags, 545
and that wallet is his wallet." 551

[1]

The con man said, "What are you saying?" 559

The president hollered, "Hush up, private. Can't you see that 569
I'm talking with this officer?" Then the president went on, 579
"This tall man is the victim of a plot. My partner is really a 593
crook. He is a con man—and not a very good one." 605

The cop said, "Do you mean that you guys are the crooks, 617
and this tall guy is telling the truth?" 625

"I wouldn't say that we are crooks. My partner is a crook, 637
but I am a president. And who would ever think that a 649
president could be a crook?" 654

[1]

Lesson 19

1

A	B
home	homesick
every	everything
under	understand

2

thigh　perk　cheat　shout

firm　delight　curled　started

different　crouch　lurk　chain

3

both　soldier　fares　truth

buddy　fooled　fellow　jacket

zoomed　sudden　trying　stared

spent　smiling　escape　sorry

common　taking　wants

4

Why Did He Tell the Truth?

When the cops said that they were taking the tall man to the　13
Happy Hollow Rest Home, the president began to tell them the　24
truth about everything.　27

The president was saying, "Yes, the tall man is telling the　38
truth. We were trying to con him out of his bags and his wallet.　52
We have also conned the woman at the steamship line out of　64
two fares to Japan. We conned a rich woman out of twenty　76
dollars, and we conned a hotel out of two hundred dollars and　88
a meal for two. There is more if you want to hear about it."　102

[1]

The cops let go of the tall man. They stared at the president. 115
The president said, "You must understand that we had to do 126
those things. We are not common crooks. As president, I had 137
to get to Japan. But now things are different." 146

The cops looked at each other. Then they looked at the con 158
man and the president. One cop asked, "What should we do 169
with these guys?" 172

The tall man said, "You may start by giving me my wallet. I 185
don't wish to be late for my trip to Japan." 195

[1]

The cop gave the tall man his wallet. The cop said, "Sorry, 207
buddy. We didn't know that those other guys were con men. 218
They had us fooled." 222

"That isn't saying very much," the tall man said. He took his 234
wallet and left. The fellow with the cart followed with the 245
cartload of bags. 248

One cop said, "I think we should take both of these guys to 261
the rest home. I think they both are not well." 271

The president said, "I don't like that kind of talk. If you wish 284
to take us to Happy Hollow, you may do so. But take a little 298
care about how you talk to President Washington." 306

[2]

"Come on," one cop said. "Get in the bus, and let's go to 319
Happy Hollow." 321

So the president and the con man got in the bus. And the bus 335
took off down the ramp. As it zoomed down the road, the con 348
man asked, "Why did you do that? All of a sudden you told 361
them everything. We both could have been on that ship to 372
Japan. What made you tell the truth?" 379

"Private," the president said, "don't talk in that tone." 388

[1]

The con man said, "Okay. But will you please tell me what 400
got into you? Why did you tell them that we were con men?" 413

"You are the con man," the president said. "And I've been 424
trying to make you into a soldier. Don't call me a con man." 437

"All right," the con man said. "Why did you tell them that 449
you were a president and that I was a con man?" 460

The president didn't say anything. He just curled his lip and 471
stared at the con man. 476

"Come on," the con man said. "Why did you tell them 487
everything?" 488

[1]

The president smiled. He said, "It all happened when that 498
one cop said the name Happy Hollow Rest Home." 507

"What did that name have to do with it?" the con man 519
asked. 520

"I have spent three years at Happy Hollow," the president 530
said. He was still smiling. "Those were the best three years of 542
my life. When the cop said, 'Happy Hollow,' I became 552
homesick." The president had a tear in his eye. 561

The con man had two tears in his eyes. But his tears were 574
not tears of delight. He was thinking that he would have to 586
start all over. He would have to plan some way to get out of the 601
rest home. He said to himself, "And the next time I escape, I 614
won't be conned into going with a guy like the president." 625

[2]

1

Hurn   mouth   ferns   sharp   air

also   breathing   hurled   fir

would   crouched   faith   Surt

poach   jerk   ouch   slashed

2

beware   except   dead   adult

toward   wrong   claws   both

stiff   two   knowing   clover

against   forward   snapped   sniffed

wolves   safe   fixed   battled   happened

sister   smelled   peered   neck   paw

growl   rabbits   floor   howled

3

Hurn, the Wolf

Hurn was sleeping when it happened. Hurn didn't hear the   10
big cat sneak into the cave that Hurn called his home.   21
Suddenly Hurn was awake. Something told him, "Beware!" His   30
eyes turned to the darkness near the mouth of the cave. Hurn   42
felt the fur on the back of his neck stand up. His nose, like   56
noses of all wolves, was very keen. It made him very happy   68
when it smelled something good. But now it smelled something   78
that made him afraid.   82

Hurn was five months old. He had never seen a big cat. He   95
had seen clover and ferns and grass. He had <u>even</u> eaten rabbits.   107

[1]

Hurn's mother had come back with them after she had been 118
hunting. She had always come back. And Hurn had always 128
been glad to see her. But now she was not in the cave. Hurn's 142
sister, Surt, was the only happy smell that reached Hurn's nose. 153

Surt was awake. She was leaning against Hurn, and Hurn 163
could feel how hard Surt was shaking. 170

"Ooooooowww," howled Surt. At the sound of the howl, 179
Hurn jerked. Then he turned his nose back toward the mouth 190
of the cave. He made his ears stand up as high as they would 204
go. Adult wolves have ears that stand up all the way. But puppy 217
wolves, like Hurn, have ears that stand up part way. Then they 229
flop forward. 231

[2]

Suddenly Hurn's ears grabbed something from the air. They 240
grabbed the sound of a padded paw taking a slow step across 252
the floor of the cave. Then another padded paw came down 263
slowly on the cave floor. 268

"Run, run," something told Hurn. But there was nowhere to 278
run. Hurn peered at the mouth of the cave. He crouched down 290
as low as he could get and looked. Then he saw the outline of 304
the big cat. The cat was bigger than Hurn's mother. It was only 317
about six feet from Hurn, and it was walking slowly toward 328
Hurn and his sister. 332

[1]

Hurn tried to back away. But he felt the hard rock of the 345
cave against his back. He could go back no farther. Surt was 357
curled next to Hurn. 361

Without knowing why he did it, Hurn showed his teeth and 372
began to growl. He snapped at the air as if to scare the cat 386

away. The cat stopped for an instant, but then it started to   398
come toward the puppies again.   403

Suddenly something dashed into the cave. It growled, and it   413
slashed at the cat. It was Hurn's mother. She had come back to   426
her puppies. She hurled herself at the cat. The cat spun across   438
and met with sharp claws. Bits of fur floated in the air as the   452
mother wolf battled the cat. Then the cat ran from the cave.   464
[2]

The mother wolf walked very slowly to Hurn and Surt. She   475
sniffed them. She licked Hurn on the ear. Then she curled up   487
next to her pups. Hurn got as close to her as he could get. She   502
felt good.   504

Hurn couldn't see that she had been badly hurt in the fight   516
with the cat. He couldn't see that her eyes were fixed and that   529
she was breathing slower and slower.   535

Hurn went to sleep feeling very safe. When he woke in the   547
morning, he could feel that something was wrong. His mother   557
was cold, and she was stiff.   563

His mother was dead, and Hurn was all alone, except for his   575
little sister, Surt.   578
[2]

1

fir churning mountain thirsty

catch sheath reach whirl bald

2

figure mind won toward

paw rabbits prodded cried

howled died scared slope

3

cool instant dead chase stream lonely

litter sniff shivering drank bank quickly

scanning fire didn't don't smelled

hungry won't rolling rounded cooking

4

The Hunter's Camp

Hurn's mother had been in a fight with a big cat. She scared   13
the cat from the cave, but the cat had won the fight. Hurn's   26
mother died that night.   30

At first, Hurn cried and howled. He prodded his mother with   41
his nose. He gave her a little bite on her ear. But she lay still. So   57
Hurn cried and howled.   61

Surt cried, too. For most of the day, they stayed by their   73
mother. They didn't go out to run after butterflies. They didn't   84
chase rabbits. They didn't even want to go to the stream for a   97
drink and a cool swim. They sat <u>near</u> their mother and waited   109
for her to get up. But she didn't get up.   119

[2]

When the afternoon sun was getting near the tops of the fir   131
trees, Surt walked over to Hurn and bit him on the tail. In an   145

instant, Hurn turned around and bit his sister on the throat. It 157
was a play bite, but it was the kind of bite that big wolves give 172
when they are hunting. 176

Soon Surt and her brother were rolling and churning on the 187
ground. For a moment, Hurn was happy, but the moment 197
passed quickly. As suddenly as the pups had started playing, 207
they stopped and sat. They sat and looked at their mother. 218

[1]

Later, when the sun could no longer be seen over the tops of 231
the fir trees, Surt ran from the cave. She ran down the slope 244
that led to the stream. With Surt gone, Hurn began to feel very 257
lonely. So he followed his little sister. 264

Although Surt had been born before Hurn, Surt was smaller 274
than Hurn. There had been another wolf born in the same 285
litter as Hurn and Surt, but she had died. Hurn's mother had 297
been less than two years old when Hurn and Surt were born. 309
They were the only two pups she ever raised. 318

[1]

Surt was the first one to reach the stream. She jumped in the 331
water. Then she began to bite the water. "Rrrr," she said as she bit. 345

Hurn ran after his sister. Again the pups began to play and 357
fight in the water. 361

"Barooo." 362

The pups stopped playing and held their ears as high as they 374
would go. The sound that reached them was from a gun. 385

Less than a mile away was the camp of three hunters. Surt 397
and Hurn didn't know it then, but one of those hunters had just 410
shot a cat as it tried to attack. It was the big cat that had killed 426
their mother. 428

[1]

The pups stood in the cold water, shivering and scanning the 439
air with their noses. Slowly the pups walked from the water. 450
But they did not go back to the cave. Something told them that 463
the cave was no longer safe. Something said to Hurn, "Stay 474
away from the cave." 478

So Hurn and Surt began to follow the bank of the stream. 490
Hurn led the way. Surt followed. From time to time she tried to 503
play with her brother, but Hurn wouldn't play. 511

[1]

Hurn didn't feel like a puppy right now. He didn't want to 523
sniff things for the fun of sniffing. He didn't want to hear 535
things just to hear them. He wanted to find something, but he 547
didn't know what. He did know that he was hungry. 557

Hurn told himself that he was thirsty. So he drank from the 569
stream. But the water didn't help. He wanted something to eat. 580

The pups didn't know it, but they were very close to the 592
hunter's camp. In fact, they would be able to see the camp 604
when they rounded the next bend in the stream. 613

[1]

Hurn sniffed the air. He smelled smoke. The smell told him 624
to go the other way. "Run from that smell," something told him. 636

But then another smell came to Hurn's nose. It was the smell 648
of meat cooking on an open fire. "Eat that," something told 659
Hurn. He felt his mouth begin to water. He stood there trying 671
to figure out what he should do. Should he run from the smell 684
of the smoke, or should he run toward the smell of the cooking 697
meat? 698

Surt helped Hurn to make up his mind. Surt began running 709
toward the smell of the meat. Hurn followed. 717

[1]

1

rounded   swirl   almost   burn

roasting   stirring   crouched

curled   mighty   Bert   hurry

Herb   Vern   grouch   stream

poach   should   jerk   grease

2

wants   wander   wash   water   watch

3

blister   scared   rustling   shines   howled

growl   stared   sniffed   pipe   spit   toward

rising   paw   fern   softly   whale

4

Surt Goes for the Meat

Surt was running toward the hunters' camp. Hurn was   9
following. As Hurn rounded a bend in the stream, he could see   21
a swirl of smoke rising from the campfire. A man was bent over   34
the fire, stirring a pot of beans. Next to the beans was a deer   48
leg roasting on a spit. Another hunter was turning the spit. The   60
men were talking.   63

"Did you see the marks on that cat?" one man said. "It   75
looked like that cat was in a whale of a fight."   86

"That cat was in such bad shape that it dropped before you   98
shot it," another hunter said. He <u>and</u> a third man began to laugh.   111

The first man said, "Come on, you guys. That was a good shot."   124

[2]

Hurn hid behind a fern. His mouth was watering. He was   135
staring at the deer leg on the spit. He wanted to dash over to   149
the spit and grab it and take a big bite from it. But he looked 164
and waited.   166

"Hey, Herb," one of the men yelled. "How long before those   177
beans are ready? I'm getting mighty hungry."   184

"Look, Vern, if you want to fix the beans, you can take over   197
any time you want. But if you want me to fix them, you'll have   211
to wait."   213

"What a grouch!" the third man said.   220

[1]

Suddenly the man turning the spit jumped up. "Ow," he yelled.   231

The man who had been stirring the beans said, "What's   241
wrong, Bert?"   243

"Some grease popped out and landed on my arm. Boy, does   254
that ever burn!"   257

"Soak it in cold water," Vern said. "Do it right away, and you   270
won't get a blister."   274

Vern and Bert ran to the stream. They ran past Hurn and his   287
sister. Hurn bent down close to the ground. He laid his ears   299
back flat against his neck. He was very scared.   308

[1]

"That water feels good," Bert said. "You should go back and   319
stir those beans before they burn. That fire is really hot."   330

"Let me see your arm. Turn it so the light shines on it."   343

Suddenly there was a rustling sound in the ferns next to   354
Hurn. Hurn turned. The sound came from Surt. She was   364
running toward the spit. She was running as fast as her legs   376
would take her. She reached the spit before any of the men saw   389
her, and she might have gotten away with a big chunk of deer   402

meat—except for one thing. She stepped in the fire. She had   414
never seen fire before. She had been in such a hurry to get the   428
meat that she didn't take as much care as she should have.   440

[2]

"Oooowww," Surt howled.   443

"What was that . . . ? Hey, look at that dog!"   451

"That's no dog. That's a wolf! And it's after our dinner."   462

Vern walked over to Surt. Surt crouched down. She curled   472
up her lip and showed her teeth, but she did not growl.   484

"Did you burn yourself?" Vern said softly.   491

"Watch out, Vern! That's a wolf."   497

Vern didn't say anything to the other men. He bent down   508
and cut a chunk of meat from the roast. He tossed it to Surt.   522
The meat landed in front of Surt's nose, but Surt did not look   535
at the meat. She stared at Vern.   542

[1]

Hurn crouched behind a fern and stared at Surt.   551

Vern walked away from Surt. "Don't turn your back on it,"   562
the men yelled from the stream.   568

Finally Vern turned to them and said, "Will you guys shut   579
up? That is just a little puppy. And it's hungry. So just pipe   592
down."   593

Surt sniffed the meat two times. Then, with a jerk, she took it   606
in her mouth. She gulped it down. Like all wolves, Surt ate fast.   619
A wolf never knows when it will eat again. The meat will stay   632
with it longer if the meat is not broken into many little bits.   645

[1]

Lesson

23

1

jerked swirled sparks chunk

watched crouched stirring snail

croaking breathed Vern burned

2

wagged group gulp hoot

sometimes owl fiddle howling

water limping paw followed Bert

sore friends orange poke want

3

Surt and Vern

Hurn was watching from behind a fern. He saw the man   11
called Vern give a chunk of meat to Surt. He saw Surt eat the   25
meat. Hurn crouched down low as the other men came back   36
from the stream. When they reached the campfire, Surt ran   46
away on three legs. She held one leg high. That was the leg that   60
had been burned when Surt stepped in the fire.   69

"Grab it, Vern," one of the men yelled.   77

Vern said, "Let it go. Do you have to kill everything you see?"   90

Surt did not run back toward Hurn. She began running up   101
the hill on the far side of the camp.   110

[1]

When Surt was about eighty feet from the men, she stopped and   122
looked back. Then she sat down and began to lick her sore paw.   135

Vern cut another chunk of meat from the roast and walked   146
over to Surt. Slowly Vern bent down and held out the meat.   158

"Are you still hungry?" Vern asked.   164

At first, Surt laid her ears back and curled up her lip. But   177
then her ears began to stand up again. Vern was very still. And   190
so was Surt. Surt sniffed the meat. Then she slowly took it in   203
her mouth. "Gulp." She ate it.   209

Vern began to stand up, and when he did, Surt jerked back.   221
"It's all right," Vern said, and Surt wagged her tail.   231

[1]

"What are you doing?" one of the men yelled. "Don't make   242
friends with that wolf. Wolves are killers."   249

"So are hunters," Vern said.   254

Vern walked back to the campfire. The night sky was clear,   265
and it was filled with stars and a bright moon. The smoke from   278
the fire swirled up like a white band into the night sky. And the   292
orange sparks jumped from the fire and followed the swirling   302
band of smoke. A group of frogs was croaking in the stream.   314
From the forest came the sounds of a hoot owl, "Hoo, hoo."   326

[1]

One of the men was stirring the beans. Another was sitting   337
near the spit. Vern sat on the other side of the fire. And Hurn   351
was trying to hear everything and see everything. But he didn't   362
move. The only things that moved were his sides as he breathed.   374

"The beans are done," one man said. "In fact, they're burned   385
on the bottom."   388

"Let's eat," another man said.   393

The men took tin plates and heaped beans on them. Then   404
the men cut big slabs of deer meat and piled them on their   417
plates. Then they ate. Hurn's mouth began to water as he   428
watched them, but he didn't move.   434

[1]

The men went back for more beans and more meat, and   445
Hurn's mouth watered more.   449

"I've had all I can eat," one man said.   458

"Me, too," said another man. "And we still have almost all of   470
the roast left."   473

One of the men went to the tent and came back with a fiddle.   487
He began to play.   491

Hurn turned his ears so that they could catch the funny   502
sounds. Sometimes they felt good. Sometimes they hurt. And   511
there were times when they made Hurn want to start howling.   522
But he didn't howl.   526

When the man began to play the fiddle, Vern lay down on   538
his back and closed his eyes. The other man sat in front of the   552
fire and lit his pipe. That man said, "That sounds really fine,   564
Bert."   565

[2]

Then something funny happened. As the man played the   574
fiddle, Surt began to walk slowly down the hill toward the men.   586
She was still limping, but she walked on all of her paws. She   599
walked over to Vern and sat down next to him. The men did   612
not see her do this.   617

Surt sniffed the air. She was smelling the meat. She wanted   628
some more meat, but she wanted something else, too. She   638
missed her mother. She wanted a friend. So she leaned over   649
and gave Vern a little poke with her nose.   658

Vern opened his eyes and smiled. "What have we here?" he   669
asked. Slowly he moved his hand toward Surt. Surt smelled the   680
hand. Then Surt let Vern pat her on the neck. Surt wagged her   693
tail again.   695

[2]

1

A	B
it	itself
bull	bullfrog
butter	butterflies

2

purple croak whisper lurking

morning soaked dream whack

thirty tail groan fern firm chill

3

knew patting washing love snapped

chasing problems wagged tugging

sneaked walking insects snooze

hopped forward tried wandered

done friends breeze doesn't tame

4

Hurn Is Alone

Surt had tried to make friends with Vern. The other men   11
hadn't seen Surt walk down the hill and come over to Vern.   23
Now Vern was patting Surt, and Surt's tail was wagging.   33

One of the other men turned around. "Hey, what's going   43
on?" he snapped. "You can't make friends with that wolf. Get it   55
out of here."   58

Vern said, "Look, Bert, did you ever ask yourself what a   69
wolf this old is doing out at night all by itself? Wolves this old   83

are with their mothers—when they have mothers. I'll bet this 94
little wolf doesn't have a mother." 100

"So what?" Bert said. "<u>Wolves</u> are no good. They kill other 111
animals." 112

[1]

Vern said, "When wolves aren't around, things get out of whack. 123
Too many of the other animals live. Then we have real problems." 135

Bert said, "Well, keep that thing away from me. I hate wolves." 147

At that moment, something told Hurn to leave. Something 156
told him that Surt was no longer his sister. Hurn was right, but 169
he didn't know it then. Vern would keep Surt, and Surt would 181
become as tame as most dogs. She would live with Vern, and 193
she would love Vern almost as much as she had loved her 205
mother. And Vern would love her. 211

[1]

At that moment, Hurn did not know all of these things. But he 224
felt something tugging at him, telling him to leave. And so he left. 237

As he did, he felt very sad and very hungry. He sneaked back 250
along the stream, back around the bend. Now he could no 261
longer see the light of the campfire. He could still hear the men 274
talking, but he couldn't hear what they said. 282

Hurn went to the bank of the stream and began to drink. 294
The water was cold, and it gave him a chill. He could feel the 308
cool night breeze cut into his fur. 315

[1]

Hurn wanted to curl up and sleep. He wanted to dream 326
about eating or running or chasing butterflies. But when he 336
was done with his drink, he began walking upstream along the 347
bank of the stream. 351

He felt like going back to the cave, but he didn't remember 363

how to get to the cave. And he remembered that the cave was 376
not his home any more. He had to find a new cave. He had to 391
find a friend. So he walked and walked. 399

[1]

The coldest part of the night comes just before the sun 410
comes up. The air is often still then, and some fog hangs at the 424
top of the fir trees. The morning birds begin to sing while the 437
frogs and some of the night insects get ready for a snooze. And 450
then the sky to the east begins to turn light purple. 461

When the sky began to turn light purple that morning, Hurn 472
was still walking along the bank of the stream. He had walked 484
over six miles from the camp, and he was very tired. 495

He had stopped only a few times after he left the camp. Once 508
he had tried to catch a bullfrog that was sitting on a log. Hurn 522
jumped at the frog, but the frog gave out with a big croak and 536
hopped from the log just before Hurn's teeth reached the log. 547
Hurn fell in the water and got his fur soaked. 557

[2]

Now things seemed so bad that Hurn sat down and began to 569
howl. He didn't know why he was howling. It just seemed that 581
howling would help. "Ooooowww," he howled. 587

Hurn must have howled thirty times when suddenly he knew 597
that something was staring at him. He stopped and sniffed the 608
air. He leaned forward and held his nose close to the ground to 621
catch any smell that was down there. Then he held his nose as 634
high as he could make it go. 641

He smelled nothing. But there was something staring at him. 651
Hurn's ears told him that. Something was lurking in the dark, 662
staring at the little wolf pup. 668

[2]

Lesson 25

1

A	B	C	D	E
set	rod	pan	bed	cam
seat	rode	pane	bead	came

2

birth crouched whined throat burp

treated attached breathed whirl

3

hollow cliff growled rolled upwind blowing

snuggled cocked scanning watching sneaked

mixed stiffly paw puffs person

goal realized asleep tugged nipped

grown yawned lasted who stood

4

The Tan Wolf

Hurn had been walking along the stream all night. Then he   11
had stopped and begun to howl. He stopped howling when he   22
felt that something was watching.   27

And there *was* something that was watching him. It was a   38
big tan wolf. She was less than ten feet from Hurn. She had   51
come down to the stream when Hurn first began to howl. She   63
had left her pup asleep in a hollow just below a cliff. And she   77
had sneaked down.   80

Now she was standing behind a fir tree, looking at Hurn. She   92
was upwind from him. Like all good hunters, she moved so that   104
the breeze was blowing toward her. The breeze was blowing from   115
Hurn toward the tan wolf. That way, Hurn couldn't smell her.   126

[1]

That tan wolf didn't know what to make of Hurn. She knew 138
that he wasn't a grown wolf. Her nose told her that. But she also 152
knew that he wasn't one of her pups. She missed her pups. She 165
had given birth to six pups. That was three months back. All of 178
the pups but one had died. She missed them, but she knew that 191
Hurn was not hers. And yet—she wanted another pup. 201

She slowly moved from behind the fir tree. Now Hurn saw 212
her. At first he just stood there with his ears cocked and his 225
eyes staring at her and his nose scanning the air. But then he 238
realized that she was a hunter. He crouched and began to 249
growl. "Grrrrr," he growled. 253

[1]

She kept on moving toward him. Hurn showed his teeth. He 264
curled his lip. He growled louder. But she kept coming. 274

Then Hurn became very mixed up. He could smell that she 285
was a friend—a wolf. So he wagged his tail and turned over on 299
his back. But he was still scared. 306

The tan wolf bent over and smelled him. The fur on the back 319
of her neck stood up. If he had moved quickly right then, she 332
might have killed him. But he didn't move. He whined a little 344
and tried to lick her. 349

[1]

The tan wolf jerked back stiffly. Then she bent forward once 360
more. She sniffed the pup. Again he licked her and began to 372
wag his tail. She sniffed him five or six times. Then she turned 385
and began to walk away. 390

When the tan wolf began to leave, Hurn jumped up and ran 402
after her. He grabbed her back leg and bit her. He was playing 415

and trying to show her that he liked her. But she did not know   429
how to act. At first her fur stood up, and she let out a growl   444
from deep in her throat. Then she bent down and sniffed the   456
pup again. He hit her nose with his paw, and then he bit at her   471
ear. She stood very still. He tugged at her ear.   481

[2]

Suddenly the tan wolf nipped him. That nip hurt, and Hurn   492
rolled over on his back. When he did that, he showed her that   505
he would do what she wanted him to do. Now she knew that he   519
would follow her to her den. She wanted him to follow her.   531

Hurn was very lucky. He was not a good hunter yet. He   543
could fight pretty well, but he wouldn't have lasted in the forest.   555
If he had been a little older, this mother wolf wouldn't have   567
wanted him in her den. She would have treated him as a grown   580
wolf and attacked him. Maybe she would have killed him.   590

[1]

So Hurn followed the tan wolf back to her den. There he met   603
her pup. He was sleeping, curled up in a little ball. Hurn   615
sniffed him, and the tan wolf stared at Hurn. When she felt   627
that Hurn would not harm her pup, she yawned. Then she   638
turned around three times and lay down with her nose toward   649
the opening of the den.   654

Hurn snuggled up next to her. They looked like two balls of   666
fur. The birds were making sounds. The sky was light purple   677
over the tall fir trees. The morning air was cold, and little puffs   690
of steam came from Hurn's nose as he breathed. And Hurn was   702
so, so tired. He blinked two times. Then his eyes closed, and he   715
was asleep.   717

[2]

1

A	B	C	D	E
bite	meat	pine	feed	note
bit	met	pin	fed	not

2

sp<u>a</u>rk   b<u>o</u>ld   t<u>oa</u>d   <u>ea</u>ting

w<u>ai</u>l   h<u>oo</u>t   b<u>righ</u>t   n<u>or</u>

3

woke   blinked   clearing   slope

moment   grown   messed   except

daytime   ready   snapped   rolled

nipped   someday   eye   scar

past   idea   yelped   different

growl   stared   shared   pack

4

Hurn Meets the Wolf Pack

Hurn slept like a log that night. He woke up once when the 13
tan wolf left the den, but he went back to sleep in a moment. 27
When he woke up the next time, the sun was high in the sky. 41
The air was almost hot, and things looked so bright outside the 53
den that Hurn blinked. The tan wolf was not around, nor was 65
her pup. 67

Hurn walked from the den, and then he stopped. There was a 79
big, black wolf standing on the slope. That wolf was looking at 91
Hurn. Another wolf, a brown one, was also looking at Hurn. Far 103
on <u>the</u> other side of the clearing were the tan wolf and her pup. 117

[1]

Something told Hurn to stay away from the other wolves, so 128
he began to walk toward the tan wolf. Then he began to run. 141

Hurn didn't know that the tan wolf was part of a wolf pack. 154
There were 8 wolves in the pack. The tan wolf had kept to 167
herself for a time after she had her pups. Any grown wolf who 180
came near her den was asking for a good fight. The tan wolf 193
could beat up any wolf in the pack except the black wolf. No 206
wolf messed with him. 210

[1]

Now that the tan wolf's pup was older, she had begun to mix 223
with the other wolves again. She still kept to herself at night, 235
but in the daytime she went out with her pup. Sometimes she 247
hunted with the pack. 251

Hurn didn't know all this. He just knew that he didn't feel 263
safe with those other wolves. So he ran as fast as he could 276
toward the tan wolf. But he didn't make it. The brown wolf ran 289
in front of him and cut him off. 297

[1]

Hurn stopped and laid his ears back. The brown wolf was a 309
little more than a year old. He was not yet a good hunter. He 323
wasn't a grown wolf yet, but he liked to think that he was. He 337
was as big as a grown wolf, and he was always ready to show 351
the others how good he was. 357

The brown wolf made a quick pass at Hurn. Hurn jumped 368
back. Then the brown wolf nipped Hurn on the back. Hurn 379
turned around. The brown wolf was quick. He jumped over 389
Hurn and bit Hurn on the side. Then he bit Hurn's tail. 401

[1]

Hurn turned and snapped. This time his teeth bit into the 412
brown wolf's leg. The brown wolf let out a high growl and bit 425

Hurn very hard on the side of the neck. He held on to Hurn 439
with his mouth and began to shake his head from one side to 452
the other. 454

Hurn started to cry. His neck hurt, and that brown wolf 465
wouldn't let go. "Owwwww," he cried. 471

His cry reached the tan wolf. She left her pup and ran over to 485
Hurn. She didn't growl. She didn't let the brown wolf know 496
what she was going to do. She ran into him and rolled him over. 510
[1]

Then she bit the brown wolf just under the eye. He would 522
have a scar from that bite for the rest of his life. 534

The brown wolf yelped and ran up the slope. Then the tan 546
wolf turned and walked over to Hurn. He was on the ground 558
crying. She licked his neck. Then she stood up and stared at 570
the other wolves. That was her way of saying, "This little wolf 582
is mine. If you mess with him, you will have to fight me." She 596
even looked the black wolf right in the eyes. She was saying, 608
"That goes for you, too." 613
[1]

Then the tan wolf began to walk up the slope, past the other 626
wolves. When she was part way up the slope, she stopped and 638
waited for Hurn. He ran up behind her and tried to hide under 651
her. She held her head up and walked on past the other wolves. 664
They stared at her as she passed. 671

Hurn felt very safe when he was near the tan wolf. And he 684
felt that way for some time. He stayed with her that fall. He 697
stayed near her in the long winter. When she went hunting, he 709
waited with her pup. She always came back, and she always 720
had food. She shared that food with Hurn. Hurn loved her. He 732

felt sad when she left. He never had an idea that someday 744
things would be different. 748

    But then one day, almost a year after he had come to the 761
wolf pack, something happened. 765

[2]

1

A	B	C	D
bend	melt	sent	gold
bead	meet	seat	good

2

<u>b</u><u>ur</u>n   str<u>ea</u>ks   sm<u>a</u>rter

<u>j</u>erked   br<u>igh</u>t

3

<u>change</u>   puzzled   jogged   smelled

gazed   showed   stared   rolled

whined   wagged   belly   grow

slope   path   hollow   darker

silver   except   checks   meaner

chasing   grown   wanted   loved

welcome   daytime   boss

4

Things Change for Hurn

Hurn had lived with the tan wolf for nearly a year. She had   13
been like a mother to him. He loved her. That is why he was so   28
puzzled that day when he came back to the den. He had been   41
hunting with some of the other wolves. Hurn was getting to be   53
a fair hunter. He had helped the pack bring down a small deer.   66
He had hunted for rabbits and pack rats. Hurn was feeling   77
more like a grown wolf every day. He jogged up the path to his   91
den, just as he had many times before.   99

[1]

But when he got near <u>the</u> den, the tan wolf met him. She 112
gazed at him in a funny way. Hurn stopped. Then he began to 125
walk toward her. She crouched down and showed her teeth. 135
"Grrr," she growled. 138

She was trying to tell Hurn something, but he didn't get what 150
it was. She was trying to say, "I am going to have pups in a day 166
or two. That means that you must leave. No more are you a 179
pup. No more are you welcome in this den." 188

[1]

She didn't look as if she wanted to play, but Hurn began to 201
think that maybe she wanted to play. So he jumped toward her. 213
She jerked back and growled louder. Hurn didn't know what to 224
do. So he started to go into the den. She growled again and bit 238
him on the back. She rolled him over and bit him again and 251
again. Then she turned and walked away from him. 260

Hurn whined and stood up. He wagged his tail and got down 272
on his belly. He was trying to show her that he didn't want to 286
fight. She didn't look at him. She stood in front of the den, 299
looking up the hill. 303

[1]

When Hurn stood up, she turned toward him and growled 313
again. "Go away," she was trying to say. "I don't want to hurt 326
you, but I will if you come near this den." 336

At first, Hurn stood and whined. Then he turned and 346
walked away. Hurn was hurt, and he didn't know what to do. 358
He didn't know that the tan wolf was helping him grow up. He 371
just knew that he was hurt. 377

He walked up the slope to a hollow where some of the other 390
wolves stayed. The brown wolf stayed there. So did the big 401
black wolf. 403

[1]

Hurn didn't know if the wolves would beat him up or let him 416
stay with them. But he didn't know where else he could go. So 429
he walked up to the hollow. 435

The black wolf was sitting on a log next to the hollow. He 448
stood up when Hurn came near. He walked over to Hurn. 459
Hurn lay down and rolled over on his back. That was his way 472
of saying that he knew that the black wolf was the boss. So the 486
black wolf let him stay. 491

[1]

To Hurn, the nights didn't seem to be as much fun as they 504
had been when he was with the tan wolf. Even in the daytime, 517
Hurn didn't play so much. He didn't want to have fun. He 529
wanted something, but he didn't know what. He didn't know 539
that he wanted to be a grown wolf. 547

As Hurn got older, his fur turned darker. At first, it was 559
silver with streaks of black. Now he was all black, except for his 572
cheeks. They were still silver. He looked a lot like the big black 585
wolf, except that the black wolf was a little fatter than he was. 598

[1]

The black wolf was also a little meaner and a little smarter. 610
Hurn found that out one day. 616

It happened when the pack was hunting. They were chasing 626
a fox. The fox was very smart. The fox would bite off bits of fur 641
and drop them on the bank of the stream. Then the fox would 654
swim to the other side of the stream. The idea was to get the 668
wolves mixed up. 671

And the plan almost worked. The wolves came to the bank 682
of the stream. They smelled the bits of fur. The smell was very 695
strong. It was so strong that the wolves could smell nothing 706
else. They ran around and around, but they always came back 717
to the bits of fur. 722

[2]

1

A	B	C	D	E
spend	bolt	tart	help	loud
speed	bout	tail	heap	lead

2

tr**ai**l   t**or**n   h**ea**ved

m**ou**ntain   sw**ir**led

3

<u>December</u>   <u>early</u>   swam   stood   rare

poor   quicker   quite   badly   lurched

bleeding   spring   quickly   drifts

tire   twenty   skinny   flowing

hungry   flowers   valley   seven

4

The Fight

The fox had a trick that almost worked, but the black wolf   12
was not fooled. He did not run around and around like Hurn   24
and the other wolves. He walked to the middle of the stream.   36
He held his nose high and stood there for a long time. He was   50
trying to get a fresh smell from the air. At last he did. He swam   65
to the other side of the stream. He howled to let the other   78
wolves know that he had found the trail.   86

The wolves had a good meal that night. But there weren't as   98
many good meals as there had <u>been</u> last year.   107

[1]

The pack was getting too big. Some of the wolves would have 119
to leave. Hurn didn't know it, but he was one of those wolves. 132
The brown wolf, Hurn, and two other wolves would not go 143
back with the pack that night. 149

When the wolves had eaten the fox, the black wolf walked 160
over and bit the brown wolf. The brown wolf howled but he 172
didn't fight back. Then the black wolf bit Hurn. Hurn did not 184
howl. The fur on Hurn's back stood up, and Hurn began to 196
fight with the black wolf. Hurn wanted to hurt the black wolf, 208
and he didn't know why. He had lived with the black wolf, but 221
something told him to fight. Something told him to win. 231

[1]

The other wolves backed away as Hurn and the black wolf 242
went at it. When wolves are really fighting, they can move very 254
fast, and they can bite very hard. It is rare when one wolf kills 268
another wolf, but it is not rare when one wolf hurts another 280
wolf quite badly. 283

Hurn got hurt quite badly. He was quicker than the black 294
wolf but not as smart. He lurched at the black wolf, and the 307
black wolf crouched down. 311

[1]

When Hurn went for the black wolf's neck, the black wolf 322
went for Hurn's belly. When Hurn curled up so that the black 334
wolf could not get at his belly, the black wolf went for Hurn's 347
neck. Again and again, the black wolf got the best of Hurn. 359

Hurn was bleeding. His ear was torn. His belly was cut 370
badly. So was his neck. But he kept lurching at the black wolf. 383
And each time he did, the black wolf got the best of him. 396

Now Hurn was starting to tire. He didn't spring at the black   408
wolf so quickly. The black wolf didn't have such a hard time   420
rolling Hurn over.   423

[1]

Then Hurn stopped. He was in pain, but more than that, he   435
was tired. He was so tired that he could hardly hold up his   448
head. His sides heaved in and out as he breathed. He looked at   461
the black wolf as if to say, "Okay, you win." But his look told   475
the black wolf, "You win this time, but I may be back."   487

Then Hurn and three other wolves stood there and watched   497
the other wolves go back to their den. Hurn knew he was not   510
welcome. So Hurn and the other wolves left.   518

[1]

Hurn became the boss of those wolves. He didn't have to   529
fight any of them. They seemed to know that he was boss.   541
Maybe they knew from the way that he had gone at the black   554
wolf.   555

Late in the fall, Hurn led the other wolves to high ground,   567
way up the side of a mountain. They would spend the winter   579
up there, and they would not have an easy time. The trees were   592
not tall, and there were not many animals.   600

The snow came early. It swirled down from the top of the   612
mountain every night. Before the middle of December, the   621
snow had piled up in drifts that were twenty feet high.   632

[1]

The winter was long for that pack of wolves, and the hunting   644
was poor. They spent most of their time sleeping. When they   655
were asleep, they didn't feel so hungry.   662

By spring, the wolves were so skinny that their long fur   673
couldn't hide their ribs. They were almost too hungry to feel   684

hunger. When they went from one spot to another spot, they   695
walked slowly. They didn't want to burn up their food any   706
faster than they had to.   711

The snow on the mountain was wet. Little white flowers   721
peeked out of cracks in the rocks. The streams were flowing   732
fast down the side of the mountain. Hurn and the other wolves 744
were on their way to the green valley below.   753

[2]

1

A	B	C	D
foam	belt	roam	mark
form	Bert	room	mask

2

nearly   mood   starved

steep   mounted

3

bothered   friendly   pretty

because   hundred   panting

dashed   somehow   followed

nape   yelp   half   hungry

growled   two   winner   woman

wouldn't   brother   tired

tried   bear   patrol

4

The Leader of the Pack

As Hurn and the other wolves slowly walked down the side   11
of the mountain, a big black bear came out of its den. The bear   25
had been sleeping nearly all winter, and it was mean and   36
hungry. The bear stood up and growled at the wolves. They   47
turned and began to walk away.   53

The bear was not in a friendly mood. "Grrrrr," it growled,   64
and started to chase Hurn and the other wolves.   73

Down the mountainside they went. The wolves had to run   83
pretty fast because that bear was fast. The wolves ran about 500   95
yards. They were panting. The bear was panting, too.   104

[1]

<u>Suddenly</u> Hurn stopped. The other wolves kept running, but   113
something told Hurn that he would run no more. He would   124
turn around and fight that bear.   130

Wolves fight bears sometimes, but that is rare. Even when   140
wolves are very hungry, they will not bother bears. Sometimes a   151
big pack of wolves will attack a bear, but wolves must be almost   164
starved before they'll do that. Hurn was hungry, but he wasn't   175
almost starved. And he didn't plan to fight with the help of other   188
wolves. He just didn't want to run from that bear any more.   200

[1]

So he stopped where the slope of the mountain was not too   212
steep. He crouched down and waited for the bear. The bear   223
stood up and began to come at Hurn on two legs.   234

Hurn didn't move until the bear was about six feet from him.   246
Then Hurn dashed at the bear's left leg. He dug his teeth into   259
the leg and ran behind the bear before the bear could take a   272
swing at Hurn. Hurn had fur in his mouth.   281

The bear turned around. Hurn stayed behind and again   290
went for the bear's left leg. The bear dropped down on all its   303
legs now. As soon as it did, Hurn lurched at the bear and sank   317
his teeth into the bear's nose.   323

[1]

Bears are funny. Sometimes they will fight, and sometimes   332
they will run away. Their noses are very tender, and a good bite   345
on the nose will make them madder or will take the fight from   358
them.   359

Hurn's bite took the fight from this bear. The bear rubbed its 371
nose on the ground. It looked at Hurn and began to think, 383
"Maybe I don't want to fight this wolf any more." The bear 395
stood up again and growled, just to let Hurn know that it could 408
fight if it wanted to. Then the bear turned around and began to 421
walk up the side of the mountain. 428

[1]

The other wolves had seen what Hurn did. Somehow they 438
knew that Hurn was a leader wolf like no other wolf. And they 451
were right. Later that year, Hurn went back to the black wolf's 463
pack. He had another fight with the black wolf. This time Hurn 475
was the winner. The black wolf left the pack, and Hurn became 487
the leader. 489

For nine years Hurn led the pack. For nine years he led the 502
wolves when they hunted. And at night he walked around 512
sniffing the air and seeing to it that his pack was safe. 524

[1]

And one night while Hurn was on patrol, the sound of a 536
howling wolf came from the other side of the slope. Hurn 547
followed the sound. When he got near, he could see a wolf pup 560
stuck in a crack between two rocks. The pup had fallen from 572
above and couldn't get out. 577

Hurn could have walked away from the wolf, but he 587
remembered something about when he was a wolf pup. There 597
was something about that pup in the rocks that made Hurn 608
think way back to Surt, and to the time when Hurn was alone. 621

[1]

So Hurn didn't walk away from the wolf pup. Hurn got 632
above the wolf pup and grabbed her by the nape of the neck. 645
He gave a hard jerk. The pup let out a yelp, but now the pup 660

was free. The pup wagged her tail and rolled over on her back   673
to show Hurn that he was boss and that she would do what he   687
wanted her to do.   691

    Hurn walked back toward his den, just as the tan wolf had   703
done years ago. And that wolf pup followed, just as Hurn had   715
followed the tan wolf years and years ago.   723

[2]

1 oi

A	B
oil	point
boil	noise

2 gr<u>ee</u>t st<u>ar</u>ved compl<u>ai</u>n l<u>ou</u>sy f<u>o</u>lded

3 <u>mustard</u> <u>instead</u> <u>wear</u> lived wanted

cheese kitchen factory settled

french fries experiment Irma

terms clothes evening smile

lazy dryer invent inventor

watching boarding Berta Carl

basement o'clock lab put

dumped second wadded women

4

Why Irma Boils

There once was a woman named Irma. Irma ran a boarding   11
house. Seven people lived in her boarding house. They slept in   22
the boarding house, ate in this house, and paid Irma for their   34
rooms and meals. But they did not treat Irma very well.   45

Carl and Herman were brothers who lived on the second floor   56
of the house. Herman worked in an oil plant. Carl toiled in a   69
meat plant. The two brothers did not get along with each other.   81

Berta was a loud woman who lived on the first floor. She   93
didn't have a job. She spent most of her time watching <u>TV</u>.   105
Three women lived on the third floor of Irma's boarding house.   116
All worked in a cheese factory. Irma worked in that factory, too.   128
[1]

Every evening, Irma came home very tired. But nobody   137
greeted her at the door with a smile. Herman would usually be   149
standing near the door. He would say, "It's about time you got   161
home. Now go out and get some hamburgers for us to eat. We   174
are starved."   176

So Irma would go out and get the hamburgers. And when   187
she would come back, Berta wouldn't say, "Irma, it's very good   198
of you to get those hamburgers." Instead she'd say, "It's about   209
time you got back. I'll bet the hamburgers are cold."   219
[1]

Then everybody would sit down and eat. And all the time   230
they ate, they would complain to Irma. "This hamburger has   240
mustard on it," Herman would say. "Irma, you know that I   251
can't stand mustard."   254

Then Herman's brother would say, "Where are the french   263
fries? You know I can't eat hamburgers without french fries."   273

Irma wouldn't say anything. She would sit there and boil.   283
She would think to herself, "Why are they so mean to me?"   295

She wanted to be on good terms with everybody. She wanted   306
people to like her.   310
[1]

After dinner, all the people who lived in Irma's boarding   320
house would get up from the table. "That was a lousy meal,"   332
they would say. Then they would go into the living room and   344
watch TV.   346

As they watched TV, somebody would clean up the mess at   357
the table. That somebody was Irma. Then maybe Irma would   367
sit down in her chair in the kitchen. By now she would be very   381
tired. But just about the time she got settled in her chair,   393
somebody would yell from the living room, "Is somebody   402
going to wash the clothes this evening?"   409

And who do you think that somebody was?   417

[1]

That's right. Irma washed the clothes. She wadded up the   427
dirty clothes and dumped them into the washer. She put soap   438
in the tub.   441

"Irma," Berta called, "don't put the sheets in with those dark   452
clothes."   453

"Yes, Berta," Irma said.   457

There were other things that she wanted to do. She would   468
have liked to watch TV. Even more than that, she would have   480
liked to work in her lab. She had a lab down in the basement.   494
She liked to work there because nobody bothered her.   503

[1]

They all said, "It stinks in that lab. Why don't you throw all   516
of that junk out?" But that is one thing that Irma didn't do for   530
them. She kept her lab. She kept the bottles, the pans, and all   543
of the other things that she needed for her experiment.   553

For over a year, she had tried to make a paint that would not   567
wear out. She wanted to do something big. And if she could just   580
make the paint, she knew that everybody would treat her better.   591

But right now she couldn't work on her paint. She had to   603
take the clothes from the washer. She wadded them up and   614
tossed them into the dryer.   619

[1]

Oh, if she could just invent that paint that would not wear   631
out! She began to think about how they would talk to her.   643
Berta would smile and say, "You're so smart, Irma." Carl   653
would say, "That Irma is a real inventor."   661

The bell on the dryer went "ding." Irma took the clothes   672
from the dryer and folded them.   678

Now Irma was done for the day. She felt good as she left the   692
room where the washer and dryer were. It was now nine o'clock   704
at night. And Irma didn't have to be at work until seven o'clock   717
in the morning. She would be able to work on her paint for at   731
least two or three hours.   736

This was the time of day that Irma always looked forward   747
to. The washing was done. Everybody else was watching TV, so   758
they wouldn't bother her. Now Irma could go into her lab and   770
do her thing.   773

[2]

1

| A | B | C | D | E |

fond   next   felt   mail   fell

food   neat   feet   meal   feel

2 **oi**

| A | B |

oil   soil

noise   pointed

3

dart   serve   around

kitchen   foolish   boarders

4

relatives   tomorrow   recall   chores

pretzels   hammer   bench   clink

super   crazy   shelf   invisible

invented   sticky   nail   upstairs

rattled   unhappy   dent

5

Irma Makes Paint

As you may recall from the last Irma story, Irma was very   12
unhappy. She worked all day in the cheese factory. When she   23
got home, she had to fix meals for her boarders. Then she   35
washed the clothes while they watched TV.   42

When we left Irma, she felt good because she was done with   54
her chores for the day. She could now work on her paint. She   67
went into her lab and closed the door. She could hear the others   80
upstairs laughing.   82

"Go get the pretzels," Carl said to Berta.   90

"Get them yourself, you bum."   95

[1]

Irma went to the jars of paint she had <u>been</u> working with.   107
She wanted to see how hard the paint in each jar was. The   120
paint had been drying for almost three days.   128

She tapped the paint in the first jar. It was not hard. There   141
was a film of hard paint on top, but the paint under the film   155
was still wet and sticky.   160

She tapped the paint in the next jar. It was pretty hard, but   173
there was still some soft paint under the film on top.   184

Irma went to the last jar of paint. She tapped it. It was hard.   198
She tapped it harder and harder. She could not dent it. It was   211
super hard.   213

[1]

"Maybe I did it," she said to herself. "Maybe I invented a   225
super hard paint."   228

She got a hammer and a nail. She held the point of the nail   242
on the paint. Then she hit the other end of the nail with a   256
hammer. The paint did not dent. She hit the nail harder. The   268
nail began to bend, but still the paint did not dent.   279

"Irma," Herman called from upstairs, "where are the   287
pretzels? How can we watch TV without pretzels?"   295

"I'll be right up there," she said.   302

[1]

Irma left the nail on the paint. She set the hammer down and   315
went upstairs. She went to a shelf in the kitchen and got a box   329
of pretzels. She handed the box to Herman and smiled. "Here   340
they are," she said.   344

He rattled the box. "What do you call this?" he said. "This   356
box is nearly empty. I must have told you a hundred times, we   369
can't watch TV without pretzels."   374

"I'll get some more tomorrow," Irma said. Then she went   384
downstairs to her lab. She said to herself, "I will test that super   397
paint some more."   400

[1]

She looked around for the nail, but she could not see it. So   413
she got another nail. She held the point of the nail on the paint,   427
and then she stopped. She felt something on the paint. She   438
could not see anything on the paint, but she could feel it. It felt   452
like a nail.   455

She ran her finger over the point. It *was* a nail. It was the   469
same nail she had tested the paint with before. She could feel   481
where it was bent. But she could not see the nail. It was invisible.   495

[1]

She picked it up and held it next to the light in the room. Still   510
she could not see it. "Maybe I've been working too hard," she   522
said. "Nails are not invisible."   527

But no matter what she said to herself, there she was,   538
holding an invisible nail. She dropped it on the floor. "Clink,"   549
it went. It sounded like a nail. She felt around on the floor until   563
she found it. It felt like a nail, but it didn't look like a nail. It   579
didn't look like anything.   583

[1]

She picked up the nail and went to the work bench. She sat   596
down on the work bench and said to herself, "I have to think   609
this thing out. I left the nail on the paint in the last jar. When I   625
came back, the nail had become invisible. Maybe . . ."   633

She was ready to think that maybe the paint in the jar had   646
turned the nail into an invisible nail. But she was afraid to   658
think that anything so crazy had happened. "Maybe . . . ," she   667
said to herself. Then she said, "Oh. Maybe that paint turned   678
the nail invisible."   681

Irma was afraid to test what she was thinking. She had   692
wanted to make a paint that was super hard. She didn't ever   704
think that she would make a paint that made things invisible.   715
[2]

1

A	B	C	D	E
food	burn	benches	pointed	load
fold	barn	beaches	painted	loud

2

soiled cooled eaten watched pounded

3

listened tests invisible copper

silver glass flatter visible

grime lazy removes relatives

freezer stomped floor stove

gallon realize shook

4

Irma Tests the Invisible Paint

Irma had left a nail on the hard paint. When she came back   13
to her lab, the nail was invisible. Slowly she began to realize   25
that the paint had made the nail invisible.   33

She said to herself, "I will test that paint." She took a coin   46
from her purse and dropped the coin on the paint. Then she   58
watched and waited. After a while, she saw that the coin was   70
starting to turn invisible. It now looked like a glass coin. She   82
could still see it, but it did not look like a copper coin or a   97
silver coin. It looked like a glass <u>coin</u>.   105

[1]

She dropped it on the floor. "Clink," it went. It sounded like   117
a coin. She took a hammer and hit the coin ten times. She   130

wanted to see what would happen to it now. The coin got 142
flatter and bigger, but it still looked like glass. She said, "I don't 155
believe what is happening." 159

    She set the coin on the paint again and waited. Soon the coin 172
was invisible. Now it didn't look like glass. It didn't look like 184
anything. 185

    "I don't believe it," Irma said to herself. She felt the coin. She 198
could feel the dents that had been made by the hammer. 209

[1]

    Irma closed her eyes and picked up the coin. "It feels like it 222
should feel," she said to herself. Then she opened her eyes and 234
looked at the coin in her hand. It was invisible. 244

    She said, "I must see how this invisible paint works." She got 256
a pot of water and heated it on the stove in her lab. When the 271
water began to boil, she dropped the coin into it. Then she 283
watched to see what would happen. 289

    Slowly she could see the coin begin to form at the bottom of 302
the boiling water. Slowly it became visible. At first it looked 313
like glass. Then it began to look like a coin that had been 326
pounded with a hammer. 330

[1]

    She lifted the coin from the boiling water and set it on a 343
sheet of foil. When the coin had cooled, she picked it up and 356
looked at it. She said, "I know that I can remove the invisible 369
paint with boiling water. Now I will try something else." 379

    She took a soiled rag and tore off a small bit. She set the bit 394
of rag on the hard paint. Then she watched as the rag became 407
invisible. 408

"Now I will see if something else will remove that invisible 419
paint." She took the bit of soiled rag and dropped it in the washtub. 433
Then she turned on the cold water and let it run over the rag. 447

[2]

The water washed away bits of grime. As each bit of grime left 460
the rag, a spot became visible. But the rest of the rag was still 474
invisible. "Cold water does not seem to work too well," Irma said. 486

Then she took a can of motor oil from the shelf. She filled a 500
cup with oil and dropped the rag into the cup of oil. Slowly the 514
rag became visible. Irma smiled. She said, "Oil removes the 524
invisible paint." 526

Now Irma had to think. She could hardly believe what had 537
happened. She went over everything five times. Then she shook 547
her head and said, "It must have happened. I must have made a 560
paint that turns things invisible." 565

[2]

"Irma," Berta called from upstairs, "what happened to that 574
gallon of ice cream that was in the freezer?" 583

Irma said, "If it's not in the freezer, you must have eaten it." 596

Berta yelled, "Well, why didn't you get more? How can we 607
watch TV if we don't have ice cream?" 615

Irma said, "You'll just have to do the best you can." 626

Berta did not say anything. She stomped back to the living 637
room. As Irma listened to her lazy boarder walking across the 648
floor, she got an idea. She smiled and said to herself, "I think I 662
can have a lot of fun with this invisible paint." 672

[1]

1

A	B	C	D	E
boiling	coach	want	pond	clod
bailing	couch	went	pound	cloud

2

sp<u>oi</u>l   l<u>ur</u>k   fl<u>oa</u>ting   ar<u>ou</u>nd   t<u>oo</u>l   ba<u>tch</u>

3

voice   recall   invisible   watched

stinky   mirror   cracked   chairs

spun   Fern   women   while

smiled   dumped   waved   buh

duh   window   listened

4

Irma Gives Them a Hand

As you may recall, Irma had made a batch of invisible paint.   12
Then she got an idea about how she could have a lot of fun   26
with that paint.   29

She began to think of all kinds of fun things that she could   42
do. She could rub the paint on herself. Then she could go   54
upstairs and pay back her boarders for being mean to her. She   66
could scare them. She could play jokes on them. She smiled to   78
herself as she began to think about the things she could do.   90

"Irma," Herman yelled. "We are trying to move the couch.   100
Get up here and <u>give</u> us a hand."   108

"Yes," Irma answered. "I'll give you a hand."   116

[1]

Quickly she grabbed the jar with the invisible paint in it. She 128
dumped the paint from the jar. Then she began rubbing the paint 140
on herself. She rubbed it on her head, her arms, her body, her 153
legs, and her feet. She rubbed paint on every part of her but her 167
right hand. Then she waited and watched as she became invisible. 178

"Irma, get up here and give us a hand. You can fool around 191
in that stinky basement some other time." 198

Irma looked at herself in the cracked mirror that was in her 210
lab. "Oh, dear," she said. She had not painted her eyes. There 222
they were, two eyes staring into the mirror. "This will spoil the 234
trick," she said. "What can I do to make my eyes invisible?" 246

[2]

"I've got it," she said to herself. She went to a shelf and found 260
an old pair of sun glasses. She rubbed the paint on the glasses. 273

"Irma, get up here right now," Herman called. "When I say 284
that I need a hand, I want you to come right now." 296

"Yes," Irma said. She picked up the glasses and slipped them on. 308
Then she looked in the mirror again. No eyes looked back at her. 321

She smiled and looked down at her right hand. It seemed to 333
be floating in the air. She waved at the mirror. "Wow," she said. 346
"This is really a kick." 351

[2]

"Irma, get up here right now!" Herman called. 359

So Irma went upstairs. And as she walked up the stairs, she 371
said to herself, "So you wanted me to give you a hand. I'll do 385
that. I will give you a hand." 392

She walked into the living room. Herman was standing in 402
front of the TV set. Berta and Herman's brother were sitting in 414
chairs. Carl was saying, "Herman, sit down. We can't see a 425
thing when you're standing in front of the TV." 434

Fern, one of the women from the third floor, was facing the   446
window, looking out. She was saying, "Oh, all we ever do is   458
watch TV. Why don't we ever do anything else?"   467

[1]

As they talked, a man on TV was saying, "Yes, we have the   480
best—the very best—cars in town. Come down today. If you don't   493
have any cash, come anyhow. We'll fix you up. We'll fix you good."   506

In a loud voice, Irma said, "You wanted me to give you a   519
hand?"   520

Herman spun around. "Who said that?" he asked. "That   529
sounded like Irma. Irma, was that you?"   536

Berta said, "I don't know why we stay here. She is all for   549
herself. She never thinks about anybody else."   556

[1]

Again Irma talked. "Here is the hand you wanted," she said   567
and held up her right hand.   573

Berta looked at the hand. Her eyes became very big. Her mouth   585
dropped open. Her lips moved, but she did not say anything.   596

Herman looked at the hand, too. And his mouth fell open.   607
His lips moved, but his voice did not seem to be working.   619

Carl looked, too. "Uh, buh, duh, buh, buh, uh," he said. His   631
voice was working—but not too well.   638

Then Fern turned away from the window. She started to say,   649
"We don't even go out to eat any more. We don't . . ." She   661
stopped talking and stared at the hand.   668

[1]

1

A	B	C	D	E
fail	painted	seal	brother	boast
foil	parted	sell	bother	boost

2

dr<u>ea</u>ms   f<u>ai</u>nted   h<u>u</u>rry

<u>ch</u>eeks   mutt<u>e</u>red   fl<u>oa</u>t

3

<u>nice</u>   <u>face</u>   voice   track   chuckle   really

ready   limp   tank   important   soaked

except   duh   buh   sense   shower

4

Did They Really Want a Hand?

    Irma had come up to give Herman and the others a hand.   12
She had made every part of herself invisible except her right   23
hand. She went to the living room. Then she said, "You wanted   35
a hand? Here it is." She waved the hand around.   45

    The others stopped and stared. They were still staring. The   55
man on the TV was saying, "Yes, friends, we have a car for   68
everybody. So come on down to the Car Mart and pick out the   81
car of your dreams."   85

    Carl was still saying, "Buh, duh, uh, buh, buh, uh, duh."   96
Then he stopped going, "Buh, duh," and started <u>to</u> say   106
something else. "I'm getting out of . . . I'm getting . . . I'm . . ."   115

[1]

Suddenly Carl turned around and took a dive at the window. 126
"Crash," the glass went, and Carl went rolling on the ground 137
outside the window. He got up and ran. He ran like a streak. 150
"I'm getting out of . . . I'm getting . . . ," he yelled. 158

Berta stood there and stared at the hand for a while. Then she 171
said, "Is that hand a hand, or is that hand not a hand? Or is . . . ?" 186

Irma said, "You wanted me to give you a hand, didn't you?" 198

"Yes, yes, a hand," Berta said. "Yes, thank you. Thank you 209
very much for the hand. Thank you. That was very nice." Her 221
face had turned white. "That was very, very nice." 230

[1]

Irma said, "Now, what do you want this hand for?" 240

Berta said, "Oh. Well, I mean—just keep the hand right 251
there, and I'll be right back." 257

Berta started to walk from the room. Then she began to run. 269
She ran as fast as a track star. Out the front door she went. She 284
didn't yell anything. She just ran. 290

Irma started to chuckle. Then she turned to Herman. "I 300
don't understand you," she said. "You said that you wanted a 311
hand. What do you want to do with the hand?" 321

"Well, you see . . . ," he said. "Well, when I said that I needed a 334
hand, I didn't really mean that I wanted a hand. What I wanted 347
was a hand. You know. I didn't want a hand. I wanted a hand." 361

[2]

"Herman," Irma said, "you're not making much sense." 369

"Ohhhhhh," said Fern. She fainted and fell like a limp rag 380
on the floor. 383

The man on the TV was saying, "These cars won't last, so 395
hurry down. Come on down right now, and we'll give you a 407
free tank of gas." 411

Herman was saying, "Well, I think I had better go now. You 423
see, I have to . . . I mean, there's a man who is waiting to see 437
me, and I . . . It's very important. And I . . ." Suddenly, he 447
stopped talking and dashed out the front door. 455

[1]

Irma began to laugh. "That was fun," she said. "That was 466
really a lot of fun." She sat down on the floor and laughed. She 480
laughed until her sides hurt. She laughed until invisible tears 490
ran down her invisible cheeks. 495

Fern woke up while Irma was still laughing. She muttered, "I 506
must have had a bad dream. I must . . ." 514

Irma was next to her on the floor. Irma said, "If you don't 527
want a hand, how would you like some teeth?" Irma opened 538
her mouth and showed her teeth. They were not invisible. 548

Fern looked at the teeth and passed out again. 557

[1]

Irma laughed some more. Then she said, "I had better go 568
downstairs now and get rid of this invisible paint." 577

She ran down the stairs and into her lab. She took off the 590
glasses and tossed them on the work bench. She grabbed a rag 602
and soaked it in oil. Then she rubbed the rag on the invisible 615
paint. Slowly she became very visible again. 622

Then she said, "I'd better go upstairs and take a shower to 634
get rid of this oil." So she did. Then she slipped into a clean 648
dress, fixed her hair, and went back to the living room. 659

Fern was just waking up again. "Hello, Fern," Irma said. 669

Fern muttered, "I can see you. I can . . ." Then she fainted again. 681

[2]

Lesson
35

1

dove carry movie place

knock face creeps tie

shrugged inside remarked

2

offering closed doesn't

bat sale drapes flipped

floating problem realize

shower pale stared started

3

Looking for the Hand

After Irma had given Herman and the others a "hand," she 11
removed the invisible paint with oil. Then she took a shower 22
and went back to the living room. When Fern saw her, she 34
passed out again. 37

Irma laughed and walked over to the TV set. The same man 49
was still on the TV. He was saying, "Before we return to the 62
movie, let me just show you three or four more of the cars that 76
we are offering as part of our sale." 84

Irma turned off the set. Then she closed the drapes on the 96
window that had been broken when Carl dove <u>out</u>. Then Irma 107
sat down and began to think of other things that she could do. 120
[2]

At last, Fern woke up. She was very pale. She sat up and 133
stared at Irma. Then she started to say, "Are you really . . . ?" 144

Just then Carl came in the front door. "Where is that hand?" 156
he asked. He was carrying a bat. 163

Irma held out her hand. "Here it is," she said.   173

"Not that hand," Carl said. "I want the hand that was   184
floating around this room."   188

Irma pointed to her hand. "This is it," she said.   198

"Come on, Irma," Carl said. "This is no time to fool around."   210
                                                                [1]

Fern ran over to Carl and stood next to him. She said, "This   223
place gives me the creeps. Let's get out of here."   233

"Not until I find that hand," Carl said.   241

Suddenly a knock came from the front door. "See who that   252
is," Carl said to Fern.   257

"See who it is yourself," she said.   264

"I'll see who it is," Irma said. She opened the door.   275

Two cops were standing next to Herman. One cop said,   285
"Does this man live here?"   290

"Yes, he does," Irma said.   295

The cop said, "I think he's flipped. All he talks about is some   308
hand that is floating around his living room."   316
                                                                [1]

Irma said, "Herman doesn't lie. If he says that he saw a   328
hand, he saw a hand."   333

The cop said, "Well, something's funny. Do you want us to   344
lock him up?"   347

"No, no," Irma said. "I think that he'll be all right."   358

The cop looked at Herman. Herman did not look very well.   369
Then the cop looked at the other cop and said, "What do you   382
think? Do you think this bird is safe?"   390

The other cop shrugged. "It's their problem. If they want   400
him, they can have him."   405

"He's yours," the first cop said, and she led Herman into the   417
hall.   418

[1]

Herman just stood there staring into the living room. " 'I'll   428
give you a hand,' it said. And then I saw the hand. It was just   443
floating in the air. And I saw it. . . ."   451

"You'll be all right, Herman," Irma said.   458

The cops left, and Irma led Herman into the living room. He   470
sat down on the couch and began to stare at the TV set. He   484
didn't seem to realize that the set was turned off.   494

As the cops were leaving, Berta came running up the front   505
walk. She grabbed one of the cops and said, "Come with me.   517
You've got to come with me. There's a hand in our living room.   530
It's just floating around. It's a hand, I tell you. It's a hand   543
floating in the air."   547

"Here we go again," the first cop remarked.   555

[2]

The other cop said, "We're going to have to keep an eye on   568
this place. There seems to be something funny going on here."   579

"Don't say I'm lying," Berta shouted. "When I say I saw a   591
hand, I saw a hand. Come inside and I'll show it to you."   604

"No thanks," the first cop said. "We've just been in there,   615
and we didn't see any hands floating around."   623

The cops led Berta inside. She pointed to the living room.   634
"Where is it?" she asked. "It's not here."   642

Irma said, "It's all right, Berta, just sit down."   651

[1]

1

A	B	C	D	E
hunt	beet	star	set	bold
hurt	belt	stare	sit	bald

2

n<u>or</u>mal b<u>ou</u>nding n<u>er</u>ve h<u>ar</u>dens

br<u>oi</u>ling st<u>ar</u>ved compl<u>ai</u>ning ba<u>tch</u>

3

<u>qu</u>iet wouldn't again bothering dazed

helping evenings kitchen bedroom

bathroom tacos grunted basement

listen chore remarked stomped

second careful face gallons

remember factory carry knock

4

Irma Gets Ready

After Irma had scared Carl and the other boarders with the   11
hand, she made up her mind about two things.   20

The first thing was that she wouldn't scare them again,   30
unless they were mean to her.   36

The second was that she would make another batch of paint,   47
a big batch.   50

For the next three or four days, everyone was pretty nice to   62
Irma. They weren't really nice. They just weren't bothering her   72
as much as they had. In fact, they didn't say much. They   84
seemed to be dazed.   88

[1]

Before Irma had scared them, Carl had eaten like a goat. But   100
now he wouldn't even <u>finish</u> one helping. Before Herman had   110
been scared, he had spent more time complaining than eating.   120
But now he just picked at his food without saying much.   131

And after dinner, Fern and Berta went into the living room   142
and sat. Sometimes they would not remember to turn on the   153
TV set. They just sat and stared at the set.   163

Irma got a lot done on those days. Right after dinner, she   175
would go down to the lab and work on her paint. She boiled   188
sheep fat. The smell was bad, but nobody yelled, "Stop making   199
that stink down there."   203

[1]

Irma mixed in a little of this and a little of that. Then she mixed   218
the paint. The first batch didn't work. Irma must have done   229
something that wasn't right. "This batch is spoiled," she said.   239

Then she began to boil another batch. She was very careful.   250
For two evenings she toiled over that batch. But it worked.   261
When she was done, she had five gallons of invisible paint.   272

She left most of the paint in a big pot. But she also filled   286
three broiling pans with the rest of it. She said to herself,   298
"When the paint in these pans hardens, I will have so much   310
invisible paint that I'll be able to make everything in this house   322
invisible if I want to."   327

[2]

Irma hid one of the pans in the kitchen. She hid the second   340
pan in her bedroom. She hid the third pan in the bathroom.   352
The rest of the paint stayed in her lab.   361

Five days after Irma had scared the others, things seemed to   372
get back to normal in Irma's house. When she came home from   384
the cheese factory, Herman met her at the door. "Where have   395

you been?" he asked. "Don't you know what time it is? What   407
do you mean by coming home so late?"   415

Berta was standing behind Herman. She was saying, "We're   424
starved. Where are the tacos? And I hope they are not too hot.   437
You know I can't stand hot tacos."   444

Irma said, "Berta, there was a big line at the taco place. I'm   457
sorry, but I went there right from work."   465

[2]

Herman grunted something and stomped into the kitchen.   473
As Irma walked inside the house, Carl came bounding out of   484
the living room. "I can't stand the smell in this house any more.   497
Get rid of that junk you're working with in the basement."   508

Irma stopped in the hall. She said, "I have something to say."   520

Herman came out of the kitchen and said, "Say it later. Just   532
get that junk on the table and let's eat."   541

"No," Irma said. "I have something to say, and I'm going to   553
say it right now. And I want all of you to listen."   565

[1]

"All right, all right," Carl said. "Say what you have to say.   577
Just make it fast."   581

Irma said, "From now on, don't yell at me. Don't tell me to   594
do every chore around this house. And don't be mean to me."   606

Berta said, "Who do you think you are, talking to me in that   619
tone of voice?"   622

"You know very well who I am," Irma said. "Just remember   633
what I'm telling you."   637

"Oh, be quiet, and let's eat," Carl remarked.   645

[1]

1

A	B	C	D	E
soil	cold	first	clean	these
sail	cool	fist	clear	those

2

A	B	C
ce	ice	face
ci	nice	circle
	race	place

3

nerve   meanest   chomping

offering   lousy   stealing

4

A	B
down	downstairs
pocket	pocketbook
up	upstairs

5

closet   warned   carried

clever   glasses   savings

pretzels   quiet   cooled   cola

keys   wise   taco   stomped

nobody   listen   bugging   loudly

6

A Chunk of Ice Down the Back

Irma had warned the others. But they didn't take her   10
warning. They yelled at her and told her that she had a lot of   24
nerve for talking to them that way.   31

Irma did not fight with them. She sat and ate her taco while   44
they yelled at her. Then she cleaned up the kitchen while they   56
went into the living room, and when they were watching TV,   67
she went downstairs.   70

She was pretty mad. At first she wanted to do the meanest   82
thing she could think of. But she sat and cooled off for a while.   96
Then she said, "I must think of a <u>plan</u> that is clever."   108

[1]

After thinking for a while, she said, "I've got it." She got a   121
pick and a hammer. She broke a chunk of paint from the pot of   135
invisible paint. She began to rub the paint on every part of her.   148
Then she slipped the invisible glasses on and went upstairs.   158

Irma was thinking, "They yell at me so much that they don't   170
have time to fight with each other. I will fix that."   181

She went to Carl's room. She felt in the pockets of Carl's   193
coat. She found his car keys. She carried the keys in to the   206
living room. She walked behind Herman. He was chomping on   216
pretzels and watching TV.   220

[1]

Irma slipped Carl's keys into Herman's back pocket. Then   229
she picked up Herman's glass of cola. She set the glass on a   242
table next to Carl. Then she took a chunk of ice from the glass   256
and dropped it down the back of Berta's dress.   265

Berta shot off the couch. "Wwwwoooo," she screamed. Then 274
she turned to Carl, who was sitting next to her. "What's the big 287
idea?" she screamed. 290

Carl said, "What's bugging you?" 295

"You dropped a chunk of ice down my dress!" she yelled. 306
"And I don't think you're one bit funny." 314

[1]

"What ice?" Carl said. "I don't have any ice. I don't even 326
have a glass." 329

"What do you call that on the table next to you?" she yelled. 342
She was pointing at the glass that Irma had taken from Herman. 354

Irma started to laugh. But nobody could hear her because 364
they were yelling so loudly. 369

Herman was yelling, "That's my glass. What's the big idea of 380
stealing my glass?" 383

Carl was saying, "I don't know how that glass got there. I 395
didn't take it." 398

Berta was screaming, "Are you telling us that the glass just 409
jumped over there by itself? Are you trying to tell us that the 422
chunk of ice just jumped down my back all by itself?" 433

[2]

One of the other boarders yelled, "Will you all be quiet! I'm 445
trying to watch TV." 449

And the man on the TV was saying, "Yes, we still have some 462
of last year's cars that we are offering—right now—at a savings 475
that you won't believe." 479

Finally Carl said, "I don't know what's going on here, but 490
I'm not taking any more. I'm getting out." 498

He stomped out of the living room. He grabbed his coat from 510
the closet. He slipped into it. He reached into his pocket for his 523
keys. "All right," he said. "Who is the wise one?" 533

[1]

"What's the matter with you?" Herman said to Carl. 542
"Just give me my keys back, and I'll get out of here." 554
"What are you talking about?" Herman said. 561
"Who has my keys?" Carl yelled. "Give them back right now. 572
They were right here in my pocket, and some wise one lifted 584
them." 585
Fern yelled, "Will you cut the noise! I can't even hear what 597
they're saying on TV." 601
The man on TV said, "Come and look at these fine cars. We 614
have one that is just made for your pocketbook." 623
Carl was yelling, "I want my keys." 630
Berta was yelling, "I hope you can find them, so you can get 643
out of here, you bum." 648
Herman was yelling, "I don't know anything about your 657
lousy keys." 659
And Irma was laughing. 663

[2]

1

A	B	C
ce	rice	placed
ci	ice	city

2

chunk   noise   tooth

outside   coins   shirt

3

argument   sure   wearing   swipe

yourself   stick   pizza   mouth

quite   quiet   slipped   aside

warned   carried   removed

front   hungry   who

4

The Big Argument

Irma had done some things to start an argument between   10
her boarders. She had removed Carl's keys from his coat and   21
slipped them into Herman's pocket. She had taken a glass and 32
placed it next to Carl. Then she had taken a chunk of ice from 46
the glass and dropped it down Berta's back.   54

Now everybody was yelling. Carl was yelling because he   63
couldn't find his keys. Berta was yelling because of the ice down 75
her back. Fern was yelling because the others were making so 86
much noise that she couldn't watch TV. And Herman was   96
yelling because Carl was yelling at him about <u>the</u> keys.   106

[1]

All at once Herman stood up. "Come on," he said to Carl. 118
"If you think I've got your keys, look in my pockets. Come on." 131

"All right, I will," Carl said. 137

"No, you won't," Herman said. "Just keep your hands to 147
yourself. I'll show you what's in my pockets." 155

Herman took some coins from his front pocket. "There," he 165
said. "Do those look like your keys?" Then he took some folded 177
money from another pocket. "Maybe you think that these are 187
yours, too?" Then Herman took the keys from his back pocket. 198
He held them up and said, "The next thing you know, you'll be 211
telling me that these are your keys." 218

"They *are* my keys," Carl said. 224

[2]

Herman looked at the keys. Then he looked at Carl. Then he 236
shrugged. "How did these get in my pocket?" he asked. 246

Carl said, "You don't have any idea, do you? You didn't take 258
them from my coat, did you? You didn't swipe them, did you?" 270

"No, I didn't," Herman said. 275

Herman walked quickly from the room. He wasn't watching 284
where he was going, and he tripped and fell against the wall. 296
"Ow," he yelled. 299

Carl laughed so hard that he fell over and hit his nose on the 313
arm of a chair. 317

[2]

Herman started laughing, but as he came back into the 327
room, he slipped on the carpet. He fell down face first and then 340
shouted, "Oh, no. I knocked out a tooth." 348

Carl laughed and said, "Serves you right." 355

And the man on TV was saying, "You can save big money on 368
these cars." 370

The next day was a very quiet day. When Irma got home   382
from work, nobody yelled at her. Carl had a big nose. He   394
wasn't talking to Herman because they had had an argument.   404
Carl wasn't talking to Berta because she wasn't talking to him.   415

Berta was not talking to Carl because she was sure that he   427
had dropped the ice down her back. She wasn't talking to   438
Herman because he hadn't stuck up for her.   446
[2]

Herman wasn't talking because he had a tooth missing. He was   457
afraid that everybody would laugh at him if he opened his mouth.   469

So all was quiet. After work Irma came home with pizza.   480
She said, "Hello," and everybody nodded. She asked Herman,   489
"How does your mouth feel today?"   495

He said, "Mmm, mmmm." He didn't want to open his mouth.   506

She said to Carl, "And how are you today?"   515

He said, "Yes, right."   519

She said to Fern, "I got the biggest pizza for our dinner."   531

Fern said, "I'm not hungry."   [1]   536

1

A	B	C	D
beach	shout	burn	soil
bench	shoot	barn	sail

2

dealing   whiter   bother   circle   face

shower   tonight   roller   complaining

3

trouble   among   false   mood

suddenly   upstairs   dentist's   rolled

dazed   forget   few   wearing

quiet   floor   argument   flying

another   sure   followed   themselves

4

Another Big Argument

After Irma had given the others a hand, they had been quiet   12
for a few days. After she made them argue among themselves,   23
they were quiet again. But on the third day after the argument,   35
Herman began to complain again. He was mad because he had   46
to go to the dentist. He complained about the dentist's bill for   58
his false tooth. He shouldn't have complained because Irma   67
loaned him the money to pay the dentist's bill.   76

Two days later, everybody was complaining again. They   84
complained because Irma came home with hamburgers.   91
"Hamburgers again?" they moaned. "Oh, I can't stand   99
hamburgers."   100

[1]

Irma said, "Remember what <u>happened</u> last time? If you're   109

mean to me, I'll be mean to you."   117

"Oh, be quiet, and let's eat," Herman said. His false tooth   128

was whiter than his other teeth.   134

"Okay," she remarked. "Just remember what I said."   142

Everybody yelled at Irma as they ate. So after dinner Irma   153

went down to her lab. She wasn't in the mood to rub invisible   166

paint all over her. She didn't mind rubbing the paint on so much.   179

But it was a bother to get the paint off. First she had to rub herself   195

with oil. Then she had to take a shower. That was a lot of trouble.   210

[1]

Suddenly she had a good idea. She fumbled around on the   221

work bench until she found the invisible glasses. Then she took   232

them upstairs. Berta was sitting in the living room chair. She   243

was sound asleep. So Irma slipped the glasses on Berta. Then   254

Irma left the room and waited.   260

Pretty soon Fern walked into the living room. She said, "I'm   271

getting tired of watching the late show. I think I'll watch the   283

roller game tonight." Then she looked at Berta.   291

[1]

Berta didn't look as if she were wearing glasses. She looked   302

as if she had two big holes in her head. You could see the back   317

of the chair by looking into the glasses. And when Fern took   329

one look into the glasses, she said, "Ohhh," and fainted.   339

And when Herman walked into the room, he saw Fern on   350

the floor. He said, "What's going on here?" Then he said,   361

"Berta, what happened to Fern?" He was still looking at Fern.   372

Then he said, "Berta, what happened?"   378

He looked up. Then his eyes rolled around, and he fainted, too.   390

Irma ran into the room and took the glasses from Berta's face.   402

Herman was still out like a light, but Fern woke up. She ₄₁₄ looked at Berta. "Oooh!" she said. ₄₂₀

[2]

Just then, Herman woke up. He reached over and grabbed ₄₃₀ Fern. He began to say, "She has holes in her head. She has . . ." ₄₄₃

Just then Carl walked in. "What's going on in here?" he said, ₄₅₅ looking at Fern and Herman on the floor. ₄₆₃

Herman said, "It's Berta. She has holes in her head." ₄₇₃

Fern said, "That's right. She doesn't have any eyes." ₄₈₂

Carl looked at Berta. Then he said to Herman, "So you're on ₄₉₄ the floor because Berta has holes in her head. Is that right?" ₅₀₆

"That's right," Herman said. ₅₁₀

[1]

Herman was dazed. He stood up and told Carl, "I don't feel ₅₂₂ good." ₅₂₃

Carl said, "And you don't look good either, but you never did." ₅₃₅

As Herman started to leave the room, he stumbled on the ₅₄₆ carpet, fell forward, and went down face first. His false tooth ₅₅₇ went flying along with a real tooth. ₅₆₄

So the next day, Herman had two teeth missing. Carl still ₅₇₅ had one big nose. Fern had a sore back from fainting. ₅₈₆

And Berta had a good sleep. When she woke up, she looked ₅₉₈ around the room at the mess. "What happened?" she asked. ₆₀₈

All of the others said, "Forget it!" ₆₁₅

[2]

Lesson 40

1

A	B	C	D	E
check	pick	tell	shot	spill
cheek	pack	tall	shoot	spell

2

price circus except peace

certain twice face nice

3

worth through arguing you'll

we'd paying smiled whistled

simmering stove spilling doctor

checked uncle's quite blush

trailers slipped cola sixth

fifth trouble once few false

quiet warned supper scared

4

Things Get Better

Irma didn't like the idea of paying for two more false teeth, but   13
she said to herself, "I think it's worth the price." One of Herman's   26
false teeth did not fit quite right. And when he said words with   39
an *s* in them, he whistled. He could say, "What are we having for   53
dinner?" without whistling. But when he said, "I smell something   63
simmering on the stove," he sounded like a bird.   72

For two weeks after the last argument nobody yelled at   82
Irma. By now Herman had two new false teeth. Carl's nose was   94
smaller. And Fern's sore back was almost well.   102

[1]

For two weeks everybody seemed tired of <u>arguing</u>. But then it 113
started up again. Everybody began to pick on Irma. And Irma 124
warned them. She pointed her finger at them and said, "If you give 137
me a hard time, I will see to it that you get a hard time right back." 154

They told her to shut up. 160

That night Irma put the invisible glasses on their cat and let 172
the cat walk through the living room. Berta passed out. 182
Herman saw the cat and spilled his glass of cola on Carl. Carl 195
did not see the cat. He got mad at Herman for spilling the cola 209
on him. Another big argument started, and Herman fell again. 219
[1]

The next day, Herman had three teeth missing. Fern went to 230
an eye doctor to get her eyes checked. When Fern told the eye 243
doctor about the cat with the two holes in its head, the doctor 256
said she needed a rest. So she went to her uncle's place and 269
stayed there for two weeks. 274

Things were quiet again, except for the whistling of 283
Herman's three false teeth. But they didn't whistle too often 293
because Herman didn't talk too much. Once in a while he 304
would say something like, "Are we having tacos for supper 314
again?" But then his teeth would whistle so much that he would 326
blush and not say anything for a long time. 335
[2]

When Fern came back, everybody started yelling at Irma 344
again. This time Irma got back at them by rubbing paint on 356
her long robe. Then she slipped into the robe and walked into 368
the living room. 371

The man on TV was saying, "We'll take anything in trade 382
for these fine cars. We'll trade for boats, goats. We'll trade for 394
house trailers, mouse traps . . ." 398

Irma walked into the living room. She stood in front of the 410
TV set. "How do you like my new robe?" she asked. 421

Everybody looked at the robe, but they couldn't see it. They 432
could see the man on TV. And they could see Irma's feet and 445
her head and her hands. But that is all they could see. 457

[2]

Berta was sleeping. Carl spilled his cola on her. Herman 467
jumped out of the window. Fern said something about an eye 478
doctor and fainted again. 482

And so it went. Every time Irma's boarders were mean to her, 494
she got even with them. But they got mad at her less often. The 508
first time she scared them, they were mean after five days. The 520
next time, they didn't pick on her for a week. The next time, 533
they didn't pick on her for two weeks. And the fifth time she got 547
even with them, they didn't pick on her for over three months. 559

[1]

Irma's boarders didn't bother her. They didn't yell. They 568
didn't complain. They seemed to be tired of arguing. In fact, 579
Herman was even nice to her from time to time. One time she 592
came home late with a pizza. Carl started to say something 603
about how late she was, and Herman said, "Listen here. She 614
works in that cheese factory all day long and still brings us 626
dinner. So stop complaining." 630

He whistled seven times when he said that. But it made Irma 642
feel very good. 645

Irma smiled at Herman and said, "Well, thank you, 654
Herman. That was a very nice thing for you to say." 665

And Herman even smiled. 669

[1]

1

police   powerful   forth   brain

race   billboard   disappearing

certainly   beard   thousands

2

audience   magician   stage   world

begun   crooks   spies   banker

gripe   griping   mind   fantastic

bottom   presto   people   woman

blanket   once   word   trouble   worth

3

Things Get Very Good

When Irma had begun working in her lab, she had hoped that   12
she would make a super hard paint. She had hoped that she would   25
become rich and powerful. But instead of inventing a super hard   36
paint, she had invented a paint that made things invisible. And   47
now she wasn't too sure about telling anybody about her paint.   58

Here's how she saw it: If she told people about the paint, she   71
would make a lot of money. But who would want to use the   84
paint? Crooks would like to use it. They could rub the paint on   97
themselves and rob banks. And nobody would be safe if that   108
paint <u>got</u> on the market. You wouldn't be able to tell when   120
somebody was in the room with you.   127

[1]

When you walked down the street at night, you wouldn't   137
know when an invisible hand might reach out and grab you.   148
The crooks would love the invisible paint, but the cops would   159

hate it. Spies would love it. Bankers would hate it. Con men   171
would love it. People with cash in their pockets would hate it.   183

Irma did a lot of thinking about her paint. From time to time   196
she told herself, "I don't care how people use this paint. I can   209
get a lot of money for it. I won't have to work in the cheese   224
factory when I sell my paint."   230

[1]

But then another part of her brain would say, "Irma, you   241
can't do that. It isn't right."   247

Then the different parts of her brain would begin to say   258
things back and forth until Irma would shake her head. She   269
would say, "Stop! I can't think about it anymore." But later she   281
would think about it again. And again the different parts of   292
her mind would say things back and forth.   300

Then one day—one very hot day—Irma made up her mind.   312
She said, "I will not let anybody have my paint. I will keep my   326
paint, but I will use it only when I have to use it. I will not tell   343
anybody about it, not even Herman."   349

[1]

Irma felt that it was a shame not to let others know about   362
her paint, but she felt that it was best this way. Besides, things   375
were going pretty well at the boarding house. By the middle of   387
the summer, Herman was no longer picking on Irma. In fact,   398
he was sticking up for her. From time to time Berta would start   411
to gripe about Irma. When this happened, Herman would say,   421
"Stop griping, Berta. She's a good woman."   428

And one day late in the summer, Carl and Fern said that   440
they were leaving. Irma was glad to see them leave. They   451
seemed glad about leaving, too.   456

[1]

After Fern and Carl had gone, Herman said, "It's so nice 467
and quiet without them around this place." He whistled five 477
times when he said that. 482

Irma was beginning to think that she had no more use for 494
the invisible paint. But then one day when she was walking 505
home from the hamburger place, she saw a billboard. On it was 517
the face of a man with a beard. "Arnold, the Best Magician in 530
the World," it said on the billboard. 537

[1]

Irma stared at the billboard. Then she snapped her fingers. 547
"That's it!" she said. "I'll become a magician. With my invisible 558
paint, I'll be able to do tricks that nobody has ever been able to 572
do before." 574

And that's just what happened. Maybe you have seen her. She 585
is called "Irma the Fantastic." And she is fantastic. She gets into 597
a big box, and they saw her into two parts. Lots of magicians do 611
this trick. But when Irma the Fantastic does it, the bottom part 623
of her gets out and walks around. Then the bottom part gets 635
into the box again, and—presto—out comes Irma. 644

[1]

She does many tricks, but the one that people come from all 656
over to see is her disappearing trick. She stands in the middle 668
of the stage. Then she rubs a magic cloth over herself. As 680
everybody watches her, she begins to disappear. At first she 690
looks as if she is made of glass. But pretty soon she is gone. 704

She lies down on the stage, and Herman (who works with 715
her) throws a blanket over her. The blanket shows the form of 727
her body. But when he jerks the blanket away, nothing is 738
there—except her voice. She talks to the people in the audience 750
while she is invisible. 754

Other magicians have offered her thousands and thousands of   763
dollars to show them how to do that trick, but Irma is keeping   776
her word. She won't tell anybody about the invisible paint.   786

[2]

1

A	B	C	D	E
truck	packed	farther	stared	spell
trunk	parked	further	started	spill

2

Salt sailor South themselves

Pacific white forty cargo

chests officer spoil match loudly

3

captain heard Rosa war

treasure younger great break

audience sunk hidden front

retired mumble listened

world tales Atlantic poke

North South relatives America

Tony twenty yakking

workers numbers shook

4

Old Salt, the Retired Sailor

They called him Old Salt, and they liked to make fun of him. 13
Old Salt was a retired sailor. They didn't hate him. They didn't 25
really think that they were being mean to him. They just liked 37
to make him mad. So when they went past his house on their 50
way to school, they would call to him, "Hey, Old Salt. Have you 63
found your ship yet? Hey—Salt! Let's go hunting for treasures." 74

"Be on your way," Old Salt would holler from his window. 85
"What do you know about hidden treasures?" 92

"Come on, Salt," the kids would yell. "Let's go hunting for 103
treasures." 104

"Be on your way," Salt <u>would</u> yell. Then he'd mumble to 115
himself, and the kids would laugh. 121

[1]

When Old Salt had first moved into that little white house a 133
year before, the girls and boys hadn't made fun of him. They 145
listened to Old Salt tell about his days as a first officer on cargo 159
ships. They heard him tell about the Second World War. They 170
listened to his tales about a chest of gold that had been taken 183
from the SS *Foil* just before it had gone down in the South 197
Pacific. The old man told the boys and girls that the *Foil* had 210
sunk in 1944, while World War II was going on. 220

[1]

"Yes, kids," he told them. "I saw the map that showed where 232
they hid that gold. A funny map it was. Everything was in a 245
code with numbers and letters." 250

At the time the kids had listened with wide eyes. But later 262
they asked each other, "Did you believe that stuff about the 273
hidden treasure?" 275

"Not me," they all said. "Old Salt just likes to talk." 286

The kids loved to listen to Old Salt tell about the roaring 298
North Atlantic Sea in the middle of winter and about how the 310
sea would break ships apart just the way you would break 321
matchsticks. They loved to hear about parts of South America 331
and the things that happened there. 337

[1]

But they would not admit that they loved to listen to the old 350
man. That's why they began to make fun of him. They made 362
fun of him so that nobody would know that they really liked 374
him. They were really mad at themselves for liking him. 384

So they called to him every day on their way to school. And 393
every day he'd poke his head out of the window. He'd shake his fist 411
and yell, "Be on your way." But then one day something happened 423
that changed a lot of things for Old Salt and two of the kids. 437

[1]

On that day a truck was parked in front of Old Salt's house. 450
Two workers were carrying a big trunk up the front steps. Salt 462
was holding the door open for them. 469

Tony, a sixteen-year-old boy who lived on the block, was on 480
his way to school with his fifteen-year-old sister, Rosa. 489

"Hey, Salt," Tony yelled. "What's in the trunk?" 493

"Be on your way," he snapped. 503

"Come on, Salt. Tell us really. What's in the trunk?" 513

" 'Tis the things left behind by the best captain that ever 524
sailed a ship." 527

"What do you mean?" Tony asked. 533

"My captain is dead. And a sad day it was when he died. He 547
has no relatives. So they're sending his things to me." 557

[2]

"What's in that trunk?" Rosa asked. 563

"A sailor's life is in this chest. Forty years of toil are in this 577
chest. The dreams of a great man are in this chest." 588

"Hey, buddy," one of the workers from the truck said. "Will 599
you stop yakking and just hold the door open so we can get 612
this junk inside?" 615

"Junk, is it?" Old Salt said. "If I were twenty years younger—" 627
Salt shook his fist at the worker. 634

The worker said, "If you were twenty years younger, you'd 644
still be an old man." 649

Tony said, "Hey, Salt, can I look at the stuff in that trunk 662
sometime?" 663

Salt stared at Tony. Salt was trying to see if Tony was going 676
to make fun of him. 681

[2]

1

A	B	C	D
limp	punch	toil	truck
lamp	pouch	tail	trunk

2

dan<u>c</u>e   pla<u>c</u>e   <u>ch</u>ill   S<u>ai</u>nt's

<u>ch</u>est   Pa<u>c</u>ific   de<u>c</u>ide   fing<u>er</u>

offi<u>c</u>er   chan<u>c</u>e   twi<u>c</u>e

3

A	B
bed	bedroom
out	outside
down	downstairs

4

<u>uniforms</u>   <u>pictures</u>   <u>close</u>   knock

kidding   limp   medal   covered

brass   ashamed   magnifying   dead

yeah   ah   code   treasure   younger

5

The Captain's Chest

A truck was parked in front of Old Salt's house. Salt was   12
holding the door open for the two workers who were carrying a   24
big trunk into the house. Tony had asked if they could look at   37
the stuff in the trunk.   42

Salt stared at Tony. He was trying to see if Tony was going to   56

make fun of him.   60

Tony said, "I'm not kidding, Salt. I'd really like to see what's   72

in it."   74

Salt turned away. Without looking at Tony, he said, "Come   84

around. Come around sometime, and we'll see what we'll see."   94

Rosa yelled, "Yeah, Salt. Maybe it's a treasure."   102

"Knock it off," Tony said. "Don't make <u>fun</u> of him all the   114

time. That stuff gets old after a while."   122

[1]

After school Tony said to Rosa, "Hey, let's go over to Old   134

Salt's place and see what's in that trunk."   142

Rosa shook her head. "No, I don't think so." Then she   153

shrugged. "Well, why not? Let's go."   159

So they went to Old Salt's place. They knocked on the door.   171

They could hear Salt walking to the door. He walked with a   183

limp. He opened the door. He stared at them.   192

"Come to make fun of my captain, have you? Well, let me   204

tell you. Me, you can make fun of, but there won't be a word of   219

fun made about my captain."   224

Tony said, "We won't make fun, Salt. We just want to see   236

what's in the trunk."   240

[1]

"Come with me, then," Salt said. Then he led them up the   252

stairs. Then he led them down the hall. There were pictures on   264

the wall. Most of them showed sailors and ships. When Salt   275

came to a door near the end of the hall, he stopped. "My   288

captain's things are in here," he said.   295

Then he opened the door. The trunk was on the floor. It was   308

open. Salt had taken some of the things from the trunk and   320

placed them on the bed. There were a few medals. There was a   333
big brass bell and ship's clock. There were two uniforms, one of   345
them with holes in it. There was a ship's log, and there were   358
stacks of papers. Most of the papers were letters.   367

[1]

Tony looked at the captain's things, and he felt sad. Before   378
he had come up the stairs, he had wanted to see everything in   391
the trunk, but now he felt a little ashamed of even looking at   404
the captain's things. Tony felt as if he were looking at things   416
that he shouldn't see. Tony felt as if he were spying on the dead   430
captain.   431

Rosa went over and hit the bell with her finger. "Bong," it   443
sounded.   444

"Ah, that's a good sound," Old Salt said.   452

Rosa picked up a stack of letters. "Why did he save these   464
letters?" she asked.   467

The old man grabbed the letters. "Don't be nosing around   477
those," he snapped.   480

[1]

When he grabbed the letters, the string that bound them   490
together broke, and some of the letters fell on the floor. "Now   502
you've done it," Salt said.   507

"I didn't do that," Rosa said. "I was just holding on to them   520
when you tore them out of my hand."   528

Tony bent down and began to help the old man pick up the   541
letters. Tony picked up five or six letters, and then he stopped.   553
He was holding a small map, or something that looked like a   565
map. It must have been in one of those letters. The map was   578
covered with numbers and letters.   583

[1]

"Salt," Tony said. "what is this?" 589

Salt could not see very well without his glasses. He bent close 601
to the paper. Then he said, "Saints be with us! It's the map, it 615
is. It's the map of the *Foil* treasure!" 623

Tony felt a chill run up his back and grab him right behind 636
the ears. That chill held on to him until his back was stiff. He 650
stared at the map. Rosa stared at the map. 659

The old man ran over to a dresser and got a large 671
magnifying glass from it. He laid the map down on the dresser 683
top and held the glass close to his eyes. "Ah, it's the *Foil* map 697
all right, with all of those letters on it." 706

[2]

Then Salt folded up the map and slipped it into his pocket. 718
He patted the outside of his pocket and said, "This old sailor is 731
going to be rich yet, he is." 738

Tony said, "Do you know where the treasure is?" 747

"It's all on this map," Salt said. "All I need to do is find out 762
how the code works, and I'll know all there is to know." 774

Then Salt led Tony and Rosa downstairs. "Be off with you. 785
Old Salt has a lot of work to do." 794

[1]

1

<u>able</u> <u>periods</u> <u>arrows</u> <u>island</u>

<u>wrote</u> window inside sure

beyond shook yeah puddles

compass chance sense during

unfold broken specks

2

spell crack numbers dotted

code thousands head nine

really ready people again

treasure great once

few because arrived

3

Cracking the Code

Tony and Rosa didn't see Salt for over a week. Salt was   12
inside working on the code. Nine days after the trunk had   23
arrived at Salt's house, Tony saw Salt outside. It was a warm   35
day. It had just rained, and puddles of water were on the   47
ground. Salt was sitting on his front steps.   55

"Hello," Tony said. "How are you coming with the code on   66
the *Foil* map?"   69

Salt shook his head. "Ah," he said, "that sure is a hard one.   82
Worked day and night, I have. And still I can't make heads nor   95
tails out of it. I think it is beyond me."   105

[1]

"Maybe you need some <u>help</u>," Tony said. "What if I helped you work on the code?" 116 121

Salt shook his head. "I don't know about that." His eyes looked at Tony. Then they looked down. "It might be that you could help." 132 144 146

"I'm ready," Tony said. "Let's take a look at that map." 157

Just then Rosa came down the street on her bike. She stopped and said, "Am I missing out on something?" 168 177

"Yeah," Tony said. "We're going to work on the code. Salt hasn't broken it yet." 188 192

[1]

Salt said, "Hold on. I don't want everybody working on this map. The more people that know about it, the more people will want a share of the treasure." 203 215 221

Tony said, "But Rosa is really smart in school. She's good at word games. And besides, three heads are better than two." 233 243

Salt said, "Well, all right. But three people it is, and no more. The three of us will work on the code. If we crack it, we share the treasure three ways. If we don't crack the code, we're out. Is that a fair deal?" 256 271 284 288

"That's a fair deal," Rosa said. 294

[1]

So they went up to the room with the captain's chest. They crowded around the table. Salt unfolded the map and laid it on the table. Then he held his glass in front of the map. "There it is," he said. 306 318 332 335

And there it was. There was an island in the middle of the 348
map. The island was shaped like a thick letter *S*. And there 360
were these numbers at the top of the map: 369

    19—19—6—15—9—12 375

    18—15—19—5   9—19—12—1—14—4 385

On the island were some letters, and there were more 395
numbers. There were arrows joining the letters and numbers. 404

[1]

Old Salt said, "If only we could find out where this island is, 417
we would be off to a good start. But there must be a thousand 431
little islands in the South Pacific. This could be any one of 443
them. Look for yourself." 447

Salt pointed to a big wall map of the South Pacific. It was 460
dotted with little islands. Most of them looked like specks. You 471
couldn't tell from the map if they were shaped like an *S*, like a 485
C, or like an *I*. All of them looked like little dots. 497

Salt said, "I think those numbers at the top of the map tell 510
where the island is. But I haven't been able to crack the code." 523

[2]

Rosa asked, "Could those numbers stand for compass 531
readings?" 532

"Not a chance," Salt said. "That's the first thing I worked 543
on. Those numbers make no sense in terms of a compass." 554

Rosa said, "This doesn't look too hard." 561

Salt said, "It must be hard or somebody would have cracked 572
the code before." 575

Tony and the others worked on the code for an hour. 586
Suddenly Tony said, "What if those numbers stand for letters?" 596

Salt looked up. Rosa stared at Tony a moment. Then Rosa   607
said, "That's it. What if the number *1* stands for the letter *A*?"   620
Salt said, "And *2* would stand for *B*, and *3* would stand for *C*."   634

[1]

Rosa grabbed some paper. Here is what she wrote: 643

A	B	C	D	E	F	G	H	I	
1	2	3	4	5	6	7	8	9	661
J	K	L	M	N	O	P	Q	R	670
10	11	12	13	14	15	16	17	18	679
S	T	U	V	W	X	Y	Z		687
19	20	21	22	23	24	25	26		695

652

Then Rosa looked at the numbers at the top of the map: 707
19—19—6—15—9—12   713
18—15—19—5   9—19—12—1—14—4   723
She said, "Let's see what we spell when we put the right letter   736
for each of these numbers."   741
The first number was *19*. So Rosa wrote *S* below that   752
number. Rosa put in letters for each of the other numbers.   763
Then she could see what it said at the top of the map.   776

[1]

1

A	B	C	D	E	F
chick	seal	fall	sprang	burn	sitting
check	soil	fail	sprung	barn	setting

2

p<u>oi</u>son   l<u>a</u>rger   b<u>ea</u>ches   s<u>ea</u>

w<u>a</u>nt   w<u>a</u>shes   w<u>or</u>n   d<u>ar</u>ted

pa<u>c</u>es   finge<u>r</u>   th<u>ou</u>sands   w<u>a</u>tch

3

sprang   flowers   coral   volcano   roses

thorns   speck   solved   sense   bunch

magnifying   glasses   treasure   pointed

sure   waves   peered   able   island

4

The Code Is Broken

Tony and Rosa and Old Salt broke part of the map's code.   12
The numbers on the top of the map said: "SS *Foil,* Rose Island."   26

"Rose Island," Old Salt said. He sprang from his chair and   37
darted to the map. "It's right around here," he said. He pointed   49
to three or four places on the map. Then he asked, "Where's   61
my glass? How can I read this map without my glass?"   72

Rosa handed him the big magnifying glass. "Here it is," Salt   83
said, and pointed to one of the little dots between two larger   95
dots. "Rose Island," he said. "I remember it well. Flowers,   105
trees, and black-sand beaches. <u>The</u> water is filled with poison   115
coral. If you step on it, you're dead."   123

[1]

"Did you say the sand on the beach is black?" Rosa asked. 135

"As black as night," Old Salt said. 142

"I've never seen black sand," Tony said. 149

"You see," Salt said, "at one time—thousands and thousands 159
of years ago—Rose Island was a volcano sticking out of the 171
sea. The waves have worn the island down over the years. The 183
rock from the volcano is black, so the sand on the beach is 196
black." 197

"Wow!" Tony said. "Why do they call it Rose Island?" 207

"Because of the roses," Salt said. "Big roses, they are, with 218
thorns as big as your finger." 224

[1]

Tony and the others stared at the speck on the map for a 237
while. Then Salt went back to the table and sat down. "Give 249
me my glass," he said. 254

Tony handed him the magnifying glass, and Salt held it near 265
his eye and peered at the map. 272

"We've solved part of the code," Salt said. "But we still don't 284
know what all these letters stand for. I'm sure that the letters 296
tell us how to get to the treasure, but what do they mean?" 309

Rosa said, "There are some numbers on the map, too." Rosa 320
pointed to the number 16. "This stands for *P*." 329

"Yes," Salt said. "There are a lot of number *16*'s on this map. 342
But what do they stand for?" 348

[2]

Rosa said, "Look. The number *16* is always next to a letter." 360
Rosa pointed to a letter. Next to it was a *16*. Rosa pointed to 374
another letter. Another *16* was next to this letter. Rosa said, 385
"The number *16* is *P*. So these letters must have something to 397
do with *P*. What's *P*?" 402

"Paces," Salt said and sprang from his chair again. "It's got · 413
to be paces." · 416

Rosa looked at Tony. Tony looked at Rosa. The old man · 427
gripped the map and walked around the room looking at it. · 438
"Sure. Paces. And I think I know what the letters stand for on · 451
the map." · 453

"What?" Rosa asked. · 456

"The letters stand for numbers." · 461

[2]

Rosa looked at Tony. Tony looked at Rosa. The old man · 472
dashed back to the table and sat down. "We can use the list · 485
that Rosa made out," he said. "The number *1* stands for the · 497
letter *A*. So the letter *A* must stand for the number *1*." · 509

"Sure," Tony said. "That makes sense." · 515

"Let's see," Salt said. He pointed to *Z-16*. · 524

"That means twenty-six paces." · 528

During the next hour, they worked on the map. By the time · 540
the hour had passed, they had filled in all the letters and · 552
numbers on the map. Then Salt said, "Now we know how to · 564
get to that treasure." · 568

On the next page is the map of Rose Island. See if you can · 582
find out how to get to the treasure. · 590

[2]

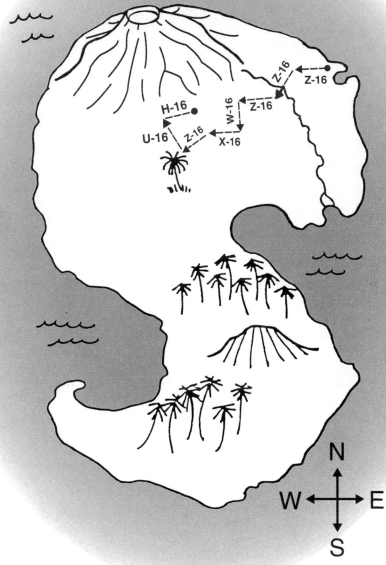

19-19-6-15-9-12
18-15-19-5   9-19-12-1-14-4

1

A	B
some	somebody
to	tonight
any	anybody

2

boiling   certain   sharply   face

straight   price   while   alarm

place   dream   load   chart

3

eight   weigh   child   whole   knew

peered   gold   island   woke   nobody

Rizzo   worth   cheek   asleep   gifts

already   tomorrow   adult   buy

4

Dreams of Gold

Now Tony and Rosa and Old Salt had broken the whole   11
code. Numbers stood for letters, and letters stood for numbers.   21
Z-16 was a code for twenty-six paces.   29

"Not a word of this to anybody," Old Salt said when Rosa   41
and Tony were leaving his house. "Tonight we cracked the code.   52
Tomorrow I'll see about getting on a ship to Rose Island."   63

Rosa and Tony walked slowly down the street. They talked   73
for a while in front of their house. Then they went inside. Tony   86
went to his bedroom and sat on his bed. He sat for a long time,   101

thinking about the map and treasure. It was <u>funny</u>, thinking   111
about a real treasure.   115

[1]

Tony felt like an adult and a child at the same time. He felt   129
like an adult because treasure hunting is something that adults   139
do. On the other hand, he felt like a child because he wanted to   153
tell everybody about the treasure. He wanted to tell his mom   164
and his dad, his little brother, and his dog. He wanted to tell   177
his friends at school. He wanted to tell everybody.   186

Think of it—Tony Rizzo finding a treasure! Was all of this   198
real, or was Tony just having a dream? Would he soon hear the   211
buzz of an alarm clock going off in the morning?   221

[1]

He shook his head and started thinking about gold. Gold.   231
Gold was something you read about in fairy tales. Gold was   242
something for wedding rings. That was about the only place   252
Tony had ever seen gold—real gold. He kept trying to think   264
about how much money gold was worth. But he wasn't sure.   275
How much does a chunk of gold weigh? How much gold would   287
be in the chest? How much would the chest be worth?   298

Tony asked himself these questions. But he wasn't sure of the   309
answers. So he began to think of something else.   318

[1]

He began thinking about how he would spend the money he   329
got from the treasure. He'd buy the best bike in town. He'd get   342
a motorcycle, too. Maybe he'd buy a motorboat. Maybe he'd   352
buy two motorboats. Maybe he'd buy gifts for everybody. He   362
could give his mother a new coat. He could give his father a   375
new car. He could give his brother a horse. He could give   387
himself five or six horses.   392

"Tony, are you up there?" It was his mother calling from   403
downstairs.   404

"Yeah, it's me," he said. "I'm getting ready for bed."   414

"Well, it's late, Tony. You should be asleep by now."   424

[1]

So Tony went to sleep. And what do you think happened in   436
his dream? Tony was trying to move a chest of gold. But it   449
weighed so much that he couldn't make it move. That was   460
pretty bad. And in Tony's dream, three people were after him.   471
They were running to where the chest was. If he couldn't move   483
the gold, they would take the chest. If he tried to stay with the   497
gold, they would catch him. If he ran away, he wouldn't have   509
the gold. So again and again in his dream, he tried to move the   523
chest. But he couldn't.   527

[1]

Tony woke up three or four times that night. In the morning   539
he dressed quickly and left for school as soon as he had eaten.   552
He stopped off at Old Salt's house and called, "Hey, Salt."   563

Salt came to the window. "What is it?" he barked.   573

"How much is gold worth?" Tony didn't mean to ask Salt   584
about the price of gold. He really wanted to talk to Salt. He   597
wanted to see the map and make sure that it wasn't part of his   611
dream. He wanted to talk to somebody who knew about the   622
treasure. But Tony didn't know how to tell this to Salt. If he   635
had tried, it would have sounded silly.   642

[2]

"That's not a thing to be talking about," Salt said sharply.   653
He looked boiling mad. "Don't talk about gold," he said.   663

"I'm sorry, Salt," Tony said. "Are you going to see about   674
getting a ship?"   677

Salt shook his head. "Don't talk about that," he said. "Just   689
go off to school and think about something else."   698

So Tony went to school. It seemed like a long day. It seemed   711
as if the three o'clock bell would never ring. But at last it did,   725
and Tony ran all the way to Salt's house. Now he would find   738
out about the ship.   742

[1]

1

A	B	C	D	E	F
coil	smell	want	boiler	deck	paces
coal	small	wait	broiler	dock	places

2

tion   nation   station   vacation   location

3

<u>parents</u>   <u>permission</u>   <u>thought</u>   <u>learn</u>

were   South   trapped   Pacific

upstairs   Wake Island   bite   minute

trying   travel   you're   didn't   who

eight   weight   treasure   somebody

4

How to Get to Wake Island

Tony could hardly wait to get to Salt's house and meet with   12
Salt and Rosa. There was a lot to talk about. All day in school   26
Tony had thought about the treasure.   32

When Tony got to Salt's house, Rosa was already there. And   43
Salt was boiling mad. Salt was saying, "You've got to stop   54
talking about gold." Then his voice became soft. "Somebody   63
will steal the map if you don't stop talking about it."   74

Tony said, "Well, I just can't stop thinking about it."   84

"Think all you want," Salt said. "But when you feel like   95
talking about it, just bite your lip."   102

"Okay," Tony said.   105

[2]

Salt led them to <u>the</u> upstairs room. Then they sat around the   117
table. Salt said, "From now on, we will write in code. If you   130
want to know something, write it in code."   138

"That's a good idea," Rosa said. "If we do that, nobody will   150
know what we're saying."   154

"Right," Salt said. "Now let me tell you what I found out   166
about the ship."   169

Rosa and Tony bent over the table. Salt talked very softly.   180
He told them that a vacation ship was leaving for the South   192
Pacific in three weeks. Salt said that he could get a job on that   206
ship. The ship would go as far as Wake Island. From that   218
point, Salt would have to rent a small boat and travel 300 miles   231
to Rose Island.   234

[2]

After Salt had told them his plan, Rosa yelled, "Wait a   245
minute. We're going to be out of school in two weeks. We'll be   258
out for summer vacation. So why don't we all go on the ship to   272
Wake Island?"   274

"No, no," Salt said. "I'll go alone."   281

Tony asked, "How are you going to lift that chest from the   293
hole? You're going to need help."   299

Old Salt said, "When I dig up that chest, I'll find some way   312
to bring it back."   316

"That's not fair," Tony said. "And it's not very smart. That   327
chest will weigh a lot. You're going to need us to help you."   340

[1]

Old Salt rubbed his chin. Then he said, "How are you going   352
to pay for the trip to Wake Island? I don't have any cash."   365

"We could get jobs on the ship," Rosa said. "If you can get a   379
job, why can't we get jobs?"   385

Salt rubbed his chin. Then he tapped the table with his 396
finger. Rosa and Tony waited. 401

At last Salt said, "That might work. Yes, that just might 412
work. We'll sure give it a try." 419

[1]

Tony grinned. He grabbed Salt's hand. "Thanks a lot," he 429
said. "Wow, thanks. Now all I need to do is talk my mom and 443
dad into letting me go." 448

"Me, too," Rosa said. "That's not going to be very easy." 459

So that's how things were when Rosa and Tony left Old Salt. 471
They had to get permission to go on the trip. But they couldn't 484
tell anybody about the treasure. 489

When Tony and Rosa got home, they went to their mother and 501
father. "Can we go on a trip to the South Pacific?" Tony asked. 514

Their father was setting the table. He almost dropped a plate 525
when Tony asked that question. "What did you say?" he asked. 536

Tony asked again. Then his mom said, "No, Tony. You may 547
not go." 549

[1]

"Come on," he said. "Please let us go. Old Salt is going. It 562
will be a lot of fun, and it won't cost any money. We will work 577
on the ship. Think of all the things we would see." 588

Their parents looked at them. "No," they said. 596

For the next three days Tony and Rosa tried to talk their 608
parents into letting them go. They tried to point out what a 620
good thing the trip would be. They pointed out how much they 632
would learn from such a trip. But after they made the best 644
points they could, their mom and dad still said, "No. And 655
please stop talking about that trip." 661

[1]

Lesson

48

1   **tion**   nation   vacation   reflection

2

A	B
pass	passport
some	somehow
when	whenever
after	afternoon
out	outfit
flash	flashlight

3   coil   waited   twice   thirty

clinkers   clearing   office

chance   during   distance

choice   furnace   season   burlap

4   sweat   weather   shovels

head   eight   weigh   tools

thought   happened   wore

dining   parents   kitchen   boiler

hired   axes   mate   ma'am

pressed   blazing   grit   grime

shower   gales   piling

5

On the Ship

Tony and Rosa tried and tried to make their mother and dad   12
let them go on the trip to the South Pacific. Then it happened.   25
Somehow Rosa and Tony talked their parents into it. Maybe   35
they wore their parents down. Maybe their parents just got   45
tired of saying, "No." But it happened.   52

Their mother talked to their father. They all talked to Old   63
Salt. Salt told their parents that he would look out for Tony   75
and Rosa. Their parents talked some more. Then, after a week   86
of talking and talking, the kids' mother and father said, "Well,   97
all right. You can go."   102

Tony jumped up in the air. He <u>yelled</u>. Rosa ran around the   114
kitchen. Then Tony and Rosa kissed their mother and ran over   125
to Salt's house.   128

[1]

And somehow the kids got jobs on the ship. Rosa got a job   141
waiting tables. Tony got a job in the boiler room. The man who   154
hired them told Tony, "This is a hard job, and I don't know if   168
you can do it. But I'll give you a chance."   178

Everything was set. Salt got the tools they would need to dig   190
up the chest. He had a coil of thick rope. He had shovels and   204
burlap bags and axes. He also had a flashlight. He said, "I   216
think we have everything we'll need." They all got their   226
passports and their shots. Those shots made Tony sick for   236
two days.   238

[1]

Then everybody waited for the day the ship would leave for   249
Wake Island. The ship would leave at three o'clock in the   260

afternoon. But Salt and the others had to be on board at eight 273
o'clock that morning. 276

It was a big ship but very old. The first mate met Salt and the 291
kids on the dock. He told them about the trip. He said, "Most 304
of the people who go on this trip are on their vacation. Our job 318
is to see that they have a good time." 327

[1]

The first mate told Salt and the kids how they had to talk to the 342
people on board. "Always say, 'Yes, sir,' or 'Yes, ma'am,' " he said. 354

The first mate showed Tony the boiler room. The room was 365
very big, and the furnace was bigger than any furnace Tony 376
had ever seen. 379

The first mate said, "This is an old ship. It runs on coal. The 393
coal is fed into this big furnace. After the coal burns, it turns 406
into big clinkers. Your job is to remove the clinkers from the 418
furnace." The first mate showed Tony how to do that. 428

[1]

Then the first mate said, "I'm going to light the furnace now. 440
In about an hour, the clinkers will start to form. That's when 452
you start working. You'll work for four hours and rest for four 464
hours. Then you'll work for four more hours." 472

The first mate pressed a button, and a fire started in the 484
furnace. Chunks of coal began to fall into the furnace. Soon a 496
bright fire was blazing in the furnace. Soon it was so hot in the 510
boiler room that Tony felt faint. 516

The man who had hired Tony wasn't kidding when he said 527
the work would be hard. 532

[1]

For four hours Tony fished clinkers from the furnace. He 542
had a long, pointed rod. He rammed this rod into clinkers. 553
Then he lifted them from the furnace. 560

After four hours passed, a sailor came up to Tony and said, 572
"Okay, you're off for four hours." Tony was a mess. He was 584
covered with grit and grime. His face was streaked with sweat. 595
His hands were sore. His legs were weak. 603

He walked to a corner of the boiler room and sat down. 615
Before you could count to thirty, he was sound asleep. 625
[1]

Tony woke up about two hours later. He wouldn't have to 636
start work again for two hours, so he took a shower. Then he 649
changed into a clean outfit and went to see what Salt and Rosa 662
were doing. 664

Salt's job was to talk to the people on board and answer 676
their questions. When Tony found him, he was sitting in a deck 688
chair talking to a man and a woman. He was telling them 700
about the weather on Wake Island. Salt was saying, "During 710
this season, the weather is fine. There are no gales." Salt had a 723
pretty easy job. 726

Rosa was working in the dining room. When Tony saw her, 737
she was clearing the dishes from a table and piling them on a 750
tray. Her job looked pretty easy, too. 757
[2]

1

A	B	C	D	E	F
reach	dock	walk	rose	show	wave
reaches	docked	walking	roses	shown	waved

2

dead   sweat   weather   head

3

stout   flowers   speedboat

location   dealing   sharply

shouting   furnace

4

crawling   wild   child   lower

scow   motor   craft   suckers

spare   interested   again

fifty   begin   deck   docked

taking   talking   eight   weigh

5

Wake Island

    Salt, Tony, and Rosa had jobs on the big, old vacation ship,   12
and it was going to the South Pacific. At first Tony was mad   25
because his job was so hard. Rosa and Salt had easy jobs. But   38
by the time the ship reached Wake Island, Tony was beginning   49
to think that he had the best deal of the three. He toiled harder   63
than the others, but his job made him very strong. His hands   75
became strong from gripping that clinker rod. His back and   85

legs were strong. When the ship docked at Wake Island, Tony 96
was in the best shape he'd ever been in. 105

[1]

The sun was boiling <u>hot</u> that day. Rosa, Tony, and Salt stood 117
on the lower deck of the ship and looked at Wake Island. The 130
ship's horn was going, "Toot, toot, toot." Other ships and small 141
boats were tooting back. The people on deck were waving and 152
shouting. The people on the dock were waving and shouting. 162

As Tony stood there, he could hardly believe what was 172
happening. His home and his school seemed very far away. He 183
had been on the ship for thirty-two days. 191

[1]

The ship had made five stops. This was the last one. It would 204
stay at Wake Island for three days. Then it would go back 216
home. But Tony, Rosa, and Salt would not be on it. They would 229
be in a small boat on their way to Rose Island. 240

That night, Tony, Rosa, and Salt were standing on the dock 251
again, talking to a woman who had small boats for rent. The 263
night air was sweet with the smell of wild flowers. And the air 276
was hot and wet. 280

Salt was saying to the woman at the dock, "We need a boat 293
that can go six hundred miles out to sea." 302

[1]

"Where are you going?" the woman asked. 309

Salt slapped a bug on the back of his neck. Then he said, 322
"We're going to look at some of the islands in the chain. We're 335
interested in trees and other plants, we are." 343

"There are a lot of trees here on Wake Island," the woman said. 356

"No," Salt said sharply, "not the kinds of trees we're looking 367
for. We have to go to the little islands." 376

The woman said, "There are a lot of little islands out there, 388
all right." 390

Bugs were crawling all over Tony. He kept slapping them, but 401
more bugs kept coming. 405

[1]

The dock woman said, "I think I have what you need." She 417
pointed to an old scow. "That is a fine boat." 427

Salt shook his head. "What kind of fools do you take us for? 440
We need a boat that is at least twenty feet long. It must have a 455
good motor. And it must be a stout craft." 464

"That's a fine boat," the woman said. "But I have others. 475
They cost a little more. I can give you a good deal on that boat 490
right there." 492

"Show us the others," Salt said. So the woman showed them 503
three boats. 505

[1]

Salt didn't take the one Tony liked best. Tony liked a 516
red-and-white speedboat. Salt picked a long, skinny boat. 524
"How much?" he asked. 528

"For you," the woman said, and rubbed her head, "for you, 539
I'll let you have it for—a hundred dollars a day." 550

Salt turned to Tony and Rosa. "Come on, kids," he said. 561
"Let's get out of here. This woman thinks she's dealing with a 573
pack of rich suckers." 577

Salt started to walk away. Then the woman called, "Wait. I'll 588
let you have it for ninety dollars a day." 597

Salt turned around. He said, "We walk ten steps from you, 608
and you dropped the price ten dollars. Why don't you wait until 620
we walk fifty steps? Then we may be able to come to terms." 633

[2]

The woman looked shocked. She said, "Do you think that I 644
would rent that boat for only fifty dollars a day?" 654

Salt said, "If you rent it to us, you rent it for fifty dollars a day." 670

It was much later when the woman finally gave in, but at last 683
she said, "All right, you can have it for fifty dollars a day." 696

Salt said, "And with the tank filled with gas and with the 708
spare tank filled with gas." 713

"All right, all right," the woman said. 720

Salt turned to Rosa and Tony. "We're all set. Sleep well 731
tonight. When the sun comes up in the morning, we'll be on 743
our way." 745

[1]

Lesson 50

1

A	B	C	D	E	F
pile	gale	blaze	mate	hire	late
piling	gales	blazes	mates	hired	later

2 head   sweat   bread   weather

3

leave   starting   once   snored

protection   reflection   chain

smooth   bounced   starter

surface   distance

whenever   flashlight

4

claws   crawling   shovels

plowed   bobbing   swells

tomorrow   across   suddenly

bananas   speckled   dizzy

head   tiny   slid

plenty   volcano   chu-cug

steered   wild

5

The Trip to Rose Island

The sky in the east was starting to turn yellow. The sea was   13
as smooth as a sheet of glass. Every now and then a little fish   27
would pop out of the water and leave a ring that moved slowly   40
and seemed to melt into the smooth surface of the water. The   52
vacation ship was dark, except for a string of lights on the top   65
deck. Little birds were walking on the beach. So were big crabs   77
with claws that could cut off your finger. The bugs seemed to   89
be everywhere. The boat was almost packed.   96

"Where are the shovels?" asked Rosa.   102

"They're packed," Salt said.   106

[1]

"What about food and water?" Tony asked.   113

"We have plenty," Salt said.   118

Rosa <u>said</u>, "That means we're ready to go."   126

Tony said, "What about gas?"   131

"We have plenty of that, too," Salt said.   139

Tony jumped into the boat. It didn't rock much, but it sent   151
out three waves. The waves moved across the still water. Then   162
Rosa got into the boat. And then Salt started the motor.   173

"Rrrrr-rrr-rrrr," went the starter. Then, "Chu-cug, chu-cug,"   180
went the motor. The boat started to move. The three of them   192
were going out into the still sea, all alone.   201

[1]

The boat began to move faster. White water began to boil   212
around the front of the boat as it plowed a path in the water.   226
Behind the boat was a trail of V-shaped waves. Tony looked   237

back at the dock. Everything was so quiet. The only sound was   249
the "chu-cug, chu-cug" of the motor. Everything else was still.   259

That was in the early morning. By noon the sea had   270
changed. Now the boat was bobbing over swells that were at   281
least twenty feet high. Up and down, and down and up.   292

Salt smiled and yelled, "This is the life. The sea—you can   304
reach out and grab it. You can smell it. You can feel it in   318
your bones!"   320

[1]

Rosa turned to Tony. "I feel sick," she said, but Tony didn't   332
hear her. Tony was looking at a chain of tiny islands. Every   344
time the boat reached the top of a green swell, Tony could see   357
them off to one side. But when the boat slid down the back side   371
of the swell, Tony couldn't see the islands any more. All he   383
could see was water, water, water.   389

Salt pointed to the islands. "Yes," he said, "we'll see islands   400
all the way to Rose Island, but we won't be there for some   413
time."   414

[1]

"How much longer before we get there?" Rosa asked.   423

"Oh," Salt said, "if we don't come up against a big wind, we   436
should be there by noon tomorrow."   442

"Oh, no," Rosa said.   446

Tony said, "Rosa, why don't you try to get some sleep?   457
Maybe you'll feel better."   461

"No," Salt said. "If you feel sick, go to the front of the   474
boat and look out across the sea as far as you can. Don't close   488
your eyes."   490

So Rosa went to the front of the boat. She stayed there all   503
day. When the sun was setting, the sea suddenly became still   514

again. The stars came out. They seemed brighter than any stars 525
Tony remembered. 527

[1]

Each star had a reflection in the water. The sea seemed to be 540
speckled with stars. 543

Tony was dizzy. He had bounced up and down all day, and 555
now he felt as if he were still bouncing. 564

Rosa said, "I'm hungry. When are we going to eat?" 574

"Eat?" Salt said. "Why, you can eat whenever you wish. And 585
you can eat as much as you wish." He tossed a large cloth sack 599
to Rosa. She opened the sack and looked into it. Then she 611
reached inside. 613

[1]

"There are only bananas in this bag," she said. 622

"Bananas are good for you," Salt said. "Eat up." 631

Rosa said, "Is this all we have to eat?" 640

"That's all," Salt said. Nobody said much after that. Rosa 650
picked out three bananas. Then she passed the sack to Tony. 661
Tony ate five bananas. Then he drank three cups of water. He 673
didn't feel hungry any more, but he sure didn't feel as if he'd 686
had a good meal. 690

Then Tony leaned back and rested his head against the 700
sleeping bags. He closed his eyes. The motor was going, 710
"Chu-cug, chu-cug." The air was cool. 716

[1]

Suddenly somebody was shaking Tony. It was Salt. Tony 725
must have fallen asleep. Salt was saying, "Come on, my lad. It's 737
your turn to take the wheel." 743

Tony rubbed his eyes and sat up. Salt turned on a flashlight   755
and handed him a compass. Salt pointed to a mark on the rim   768
of the compass. "Keep the front of the boat pointing at this   780
mark. This will take us straight to Rose Island."   789

So Tony took the wheel and steered the boat. Salt curled up   801
in the back of the boat and went to sleep. He snored very   814
loudly. Rosa was sleeping in the front of the boat. The air was   827
cool now, and everything was quiet.   833

[1]

1

A	B	C	D	E
tape	soak	tire	whack	sweat
taped	soaking	tired	whacks	sweats

2

A	B
under	underbrush
land	landmark
after	afternoon

3

reflec<u>tion</u>   ac<u>cor</u>ding   b<u>oi</u>l

protec<u>tion</u>   c<u>ur</u>l

4

<u>machete</u>   <u>fortune</u>   <u>engine</u>   <u>climb</u>   <u>juice</u>

rim   across   choppy   spray   bobbing

cliffs   cove   dizzy   jungle   speck

wobbly   shore   realized   tangle

calm   against   clear   volcano   through

5

Rose Island at Last

Tony steered the boat most of the night. When the sky began   12
to grow light, the sea became choppy again. Each time the   23
front of the boat went through a wave, water sprayed into the   35
air. Some of it landed in the boat.   43

"Hey," Rosa said, "turn the boat so that it doesn't make so   55
much spray."   57

Old Salt jumped up from the back of the boat. "You'd have   69
Tony do that?" he yelled. "You'd have him miss Rose Island   80
after we've come all this way?"   86

"No," Rosa said. "I'm just getting tired of getting wet."   96
                                                            [1]

Salt smiled. A wave with a curl of white water slapped the   108
front of the boat. Rosa was soaked. Salt was soaked, but <u>he</u> kept 121
on smiling. Then he said, "There she be. There be Rose Island." 133

Tony tried to stand up. But the boat was bobbing so much   145
that it knocked Tony down.   150

"We're there," Salt said. "We'll be on dry land before you   161
know it."   163

Two hours later, the boat was next to the island. They hadn't   175
landed yet, but they were near the cove on the north end of the 189
island. Tony watched the waves dash against the high cliffs of   200
the island.   202
                                                            [1]

The island didn't look the way Tony had thought it would. It   214
looked much bigger than he had thought. And the cliffs were   225
much higher than he had thought.   231

At last, the boat came to a place where there were no cliffs.   244
There was a little cove. The water in the cove was clear and very 258
green. Tony could see fish swimming under the surface of the   269
water. The boat slid up on the black-sand beach. Salt cut the   281
engine, and everything was calm, except for the hooting of birds. 292

"All right," Salt said. "Grab the tools and let's be off to find 305
our fortune of gold."   309
                                                            [1]

Tony grabbed three shovels and a coil of rope. When he   320
began to walk across the beach, he realized that he was dizzy.   332
It felt as if the beach were rolling this way and that way.   345

Rosa said, "Tony, you walk the way I feel. I'm dizzy."   356

Old Salt laughed. "You'll be a little wobbly for a few hours,   368
but you'll get over it."   373

Tony followed Salt up a large hill. When they got to the top,   386
Tony was out of wind. He looked back down the hill. The boat   399
looked like a tiny speck on the shore of the cove.   410

[1]

"We've come a long way," Tony said.   417

"Not on the map, we haven't," Salt said. "We have gone up a   430
lot, but we haven't gone very far from the shore." Salt took out   443
the map. "We're at the rim of the hill now. So we can start   457
pacing." He rubbed his chin. "According to the map," he said,   468
"we should start pacing from a place that is a little north of the   482
cove and east of the volcano. But I can't see the volcano. All I   496
can see is a jungle."   501

Salt was right. To the west there was nothing but a tangle of   514
green vines and trees. Beneath the trees were plants with leaves   525
bigger than Tony.   528

[1]

"I'll have to climb a tree," Salt said. And he did. He found a   542
tall tree near the rim of the hill. The tree had heavy vines   555
growing around its trunk. Salt climbed all the way to the top.   567
Then he locked his legs around the tree, took out his compass,   579
and looked at it.   583

Salt yelled, "Go about three hundred feet north of here."   594
Tony and Rosa ran north along the rim of the hill.   605

"That's good," Salt said.   609

[1]

Then Salt climbed back down the tree like a monkey. He ran   621
up to them, pointed toward the jungle, and said, "We go that   633
way twenty-six paces."   636

So they began to walk. Salt went first. He took out a large   649
machete and whacked a path through the underbrush. The air   659
felt wet in the jungle. And the plants spit out juice when Salt's   672
machete cut through them. Tony was sweating. So were the   682
others.   683

"Twenty-five . . . twenty-six," Salt said, and stopped.   689

Then he turned to Rosa. "You stand on this spot. Tony and I   702
will look for a landmark. If we can't find a landmark, we won't   715
know if we are too far north or too far south."   726

[1]

Salt handed a machete to Tony. Salt said, "Cut a path south.   738
Be careful of the plants. Some of them have thorns and sharp   750
blades."   751

Tony went south. Salt went north. Tony had gone about   761
thirty feet when he came to a large rock. It was twice as tall as   776
Tony, and it was covered with moss.   783

"I think I've found a landmark," Tony called.   791

Salt came running through the jungle. He smiled. The sweat   801
was streaming down his face. He slapped the rock. "So you   812
did, my boy. You found a real landmark. This is what we're   824
looking for. It won't be long now before we reach the treasure."   836

[1]

1

A	B	C
ge	engine	ledge
gi	edge	huge
	bridge	change
	large	strange

2

excited   coil   filtered   fallen   curl   first

3

A	B
sun	sunlight
under	underbrush
south	southwest

4

ocean   knot   course   heart   few

grew   due   machete   fortune

wild   white   bare   world   trunk

dense   stream   jungle   arrows

squinted   beetle   rotting   twist   moment

full   tied   throw   sure   ferns

5

More Landmarks

Everything was green inside the jungle. Even the light was   10
green. Tony's white shirt looked green. No sunlight got   19
through the dense trees. Only a green glow filtered down to the   31
floor of the jungle.   35

Salt was leading the way. Tony followed. Then came Rosa.   45
After they reached the huge, moss-covered rock, they turned   54
slightly to the south and paced off another twenty-six paces.   64
They stopped at the edge of the stream. They jumped across the   76
stream, turned more toward the west, and paced off another   86
twenty-six paces. They stopped at the edge of a very steep slope.   98
[1]

"This must be the foot of the volcano," Salt said. "So far   110
we've been lucky. There has been a landmark for <u>every</u> arrow   121
on the map."   124

Now Salt and the others turned south. The map said *W-16*.   136
So Salt stepped off twenty-three paces and stopped. There was   146
no landmark.   148

Salt mopped the sweat from his face. He squinted and   158
looked through the underbrush. "No landmark," he said. "But   167
let's go on. We know that we were going right when we got to   181
the foot of the volcano."   186

The next arrow on the map was pointing due west. The map said   199
X-16. "Twenty-four paces," Salt said and began to step them off.   211
[1]

When Salt stopped, he looked around. Tony and Rosa   220
looked around. No landmark. Salt shook his head. The jungle   230
was not as dense as it had been. There were a few plants. Most   244

of them were huge ferns. It would have been easy to see a 257
landmark. But there was none. 262

"What should we do?" Tony asked. 268

Salt ran his sleeve across his face. "What should we do? Do 280
you think we came across the ocean so that we could stop here? 293
We're going on. That's what we're going to do!" 302

Salt took out his compass, turned to the southwest, and checked 313
the map. "Twenty-six paces," he said and began to step them off. 325

[1]

When Salt stopped he shook his head. No landmark was in sight. 337

"This doesn't look good. We'll find that treasure, all right. 347
But we may have gone off course back there." 356

With that, Salt sat down on the ground. The ground was 367
almost bare. And it was wet, as Tony found out when he sat down. 381

Suddenly a big beetle, almost as big as your fist, darted 392
across Tony's leg. Tony jumped up. "What was that?" he yelled. 403
He could feel his heart pounding in his ears. 412

[1]

Salt laughed. "That, my boy, is what we call a bug. It's not a 426
big bug for this part of the world, but it's a bug just the same. 441
And we'll be living with lots of bugs for the next few days." 454

Tony almost said, "Let's go back. Let's forget about the gold 465
and get out of here." But he knew that it would be silly to leave 480
when they were so close to the treasure. So he didn't say anything. 493

Tony didn't want to sit on the ground any more. So he 505
looked around for something else to sit on. He saw a fallen tree 518
trunk a few feet from the others. 525

[1]

But when Tony walked over to the tree trunk, he didn't like 537
the way it looked. It was rotting and falling apart. It looked as if 551

it were full of all kinds of bugs. And it had a strange twist in the [567] trunk. The trunk looked as if somebody had tied it into a knot. [580]

A knot in the trunk of an old tree—it took Tony a moment [594] to realize what that could mean. [600]

"Hey," Tony yelled. "I found a landmark. Come here." The [610] others ran over to the fallen tree. "Look at the trunk," Tony said. [623]

[1]

"Sure," Salt said. "It's a mark all right. It was a young tree at the [638] time they tied a knot in the trunk. The tree grew bigger and bigger. [652] Then it died and fell over. In a few years there won't be anything [666] left of it. But there it is, the landmark. We're right on course." [679]

Tony walked to the roots of the old tree. He took out his [692] compass and looked at the map. "U-sixteen," he said. "That [703] means twenty-one paces." [706]

Salt stepped them off. He stopped at the foot of a steep hill. [719] Tony felt very excited. He knew the map by heart. He knew [731] that there was one more arrow before the treasure—*H-16*. [742]

[1]

Tony didn't wait for Salt. He began to pace off eight paces to [755] the east. He stopped in front of a large pile of rocks. [767]

"This is it," he hollered. "We found the treasure. It's under [778] this pile of rocks." [782]

He ran over and threw his arms around Rosa. Rosa was [793] soaking wet. "We did it, Rosa," he said. "We're rich." [803]

"Not yet, we're not," Salt said. "We're not rich until we get [815] that treasure out of the ground." [821]

Rosa said, "But we've already done the hard part. The rest is [833] going to be easy." [837]

"No, it won't," Salt said. "Our real work has just begun." [848]

[1]

1

A	B	C
ge	huge	stranger
gi	engine	bridge
	change	germ
	gentle	budge

2

protec<u>tion</u>   cle<u>v</u>er   h<u>ea</u>ved   <u>it</u>ched

cra<u>sh</u>ing   unc<u>oi</u>led   cr<u>ou</u>ched   <u>ch</u>ir<u>p</u>ing

selec<u>tion</u>   distan<u>c</u>e   vaca<u>tion</u>   c<u>oo</u>ler

3

<u>pulled</u>   <u>rough</u>   <u>enough</u>   <u>hauled</u>   <u>knife</u>

<u>touch</u>   knot   moment   beginning

probably   handle   minute   blade   allowed

flies   level   sunset   rattling   tackled

rumbling   distant   sore   rusty

tugged   realize   underbrush   bites

ocean   course   machete   biting   tumbled

4

Digging for Gold

Tony's hands were sore. His back was sore. So were his legs.   12
He was beginning to realize that Salt had been right when he'd   24
said that the real work was just beginning. For the past three   36
hours, Tony had hauled rocks from the pile. At first the pile had   49
been about six feet high. Now it was only about one foot high.   62

Tony bent down and grabbed another rock. When he picked   72
it up, he saw something below it. "Hey, Rosa," he said. "What's   84
that?"   85

Rosa tossed a rock into the underbrush. Then she wiped the   96
sweat from her eyes. She bent down and looked where Tony   107
was pointing. "It looks like a knife handle," Rosa said. "I'll   118
pull it out."   121

[1]

Rosa was about to grab the handle when Salt tackled her.   132
"No," Salt yelled. Salt and Rosa tumbled over the rock pile.   143
Then Salt sat up and said, "Don't touch it. It may be a trap."   157

"What do you mean?" Rosa asked. Rosa was rubbing her arm.   168

Salt said, "If you had a treasure in the ground, would you   180
leave it without some kind of protection?"   187

"I don't know," Rosa said.   192

[1]

"Well, the people who put this treasure in the ground   202
wouldn't do that," Salt said. "They wouldn't want some   211
stranger to come along and take their treasure. So they   221
probably fixed a trap. If anybody pulls out that handle, the   232
trap goes off. And the stranger won't have to worry about   243
hauling the treasure home. The stranger will be dead."   252

"How does the trap work?" Tony asked.   259

"I don't know," Salt said. "Go get the rope, and we'll find out."   272

Tony ran and got the coil of rope. He gave it to Salt. Salt   286
uncoiled the rope and tied one end of it around the handle of   299
the knife. Then Salt stepped back about twenty paces.   308

[1]

"Get back," he said. "When I pull this rope, there is no   320
telling what will happen."   324

Tony and Rosa ran far back into the jungle. They crouched 335
down behind a large tree. The tree was covered with bugs, but 347
they didn't seem to care. They were watching Salt. 356

"Here it goes," Salt said. He tugged on the rope. Nothing 367
happened. The knife didn't budge. He tugged the knife again 377
and again and again. 381

Suddenly the knife came out of the ground. And just as 392
suddenly there was a rumbling sound up the side of the 403
volcano. The sound was followed by a huge pile of rocks. 414
Down they came. They landed right where Tony and Rosa had 425
been standing. 427

[1]

Tony shook his head and brushed a big beetle from his arm. 439
"Wow," he said. "And to think that I was standing there a 451
minute ago." 453

Rosa called, "Is it all right to come out now?" 463

"Yes, yes," Salt said. "It's time to come out and haul some 475
more rocks from the pile." The pile was now about six feet high 488
again. 489

"How did they do that?" Tony asked. 496

"It was pretty clever," Salt said. He held up the knife handle. 508
There was no blade attached to the handle. There was an old, 520
rusty chain. 522

[1]

Salt said, "That chain led to a pile of rocks up the side of the 537
volcano. When I pulled on the chain, I pulled the bottom rock 549
out. That allowed the other rocks to fall down." 558

So Tony and Rosa went back to the rock pile and heaved 570
rocks. They were almost finished when the forest began to 580
grow dark. And when the forest began to grow dark, flies and 592

other biting bugs came out. They came in clouds. It was hard 604
for Tony to work. He spent most of his time slapping bugs. 616
They bit through his shirt and pants. Most of the bites itched. 628
Some of them hurt. 632

[1]

"I can't take much more of this," Tony said. 641

"Neither can I," Salt said. "Let's go where the bugs don't like 653
to go." 655

"Where's that?" Rosa asked. 659

"Up the volcano," Salt said. "There should be a good breeze 670
up there, if we go high enough. And it should be cooler up 683
there." 684

So Salt, Rosa, and Tony began to climb the volcano. Tony 695
was tired. But he didn't mind climbing the volcano. He didn't 706
mind anything that would get rid of those bugs. 715

[1]

At last Salt came to a level spot. The breeze was blowing. 727
The air was cool. Off in the distance, Tony could see the sunset 740
and the sea. It was rough, with huge white caps rolling against 752
the cliffs. 754

Suddenly, Tony began to shake. "I'm cold," he said. 763

Salt said, "Just lie down and close your eyes. In a few 775
moments you'll feel fine. You'll feel real fine." 783

So Tony lay back and closed his eyes. He could hear the 795
sound of the distant waves crashing against the cliffs of Rose 806
Island. He could hear the breeze rattling leaves in the trees. He 818
could hear the night birds chirping. He felt very, very tired. 829
Very tired. 831

[1]

1 knife   know   knock   knot   knew

2

A	B	C
ge	edge	range
gi	change	magic
	large	charge
	ledge	strange

3 couple   brought   pushed   breakfast

bananas   yesterday   coffee   clever

rusty   swallows   shovels   enough

rough   hauled   found   wrong

4 pulled   bitter   soil   bare

thousands   chunks   corner   coin

morning   drank   clink   gone

5

Where Is the Treasure Chest?

When Tony woke up, he smelled smoke. He looked around.   10
There was Salt cooking something over a fire. "What are we   21
having for breakfast?" Tony asked.   26

"It's a fine breakfast you'll have," Salt said. "Bananas and   36
coffee."   37

"Oh," Tony said. He wasn't very hungry for any more   47
bananas. He could still taste the bananas he'd eaten yesterday   57
and the day before. But bananas were better than nothing. So   68
Tony ate three bananas and tried to drink some of the coffee   80
Salt fixed. That coffee was so bitter that Tony couldn't drink   91
more than a few swallows.   96

[1]

But there was one good thing about the coffee. After you   107
drank some of it, you couldn't taste bananas any more. All you   119
could taste was coffee. And you could taste coffee all morning.   130

The taste hadn't left Tony's mouth by the time they reached   141
the foot of the volcano. It hadn't gone away when Tony and   153
Rosa started to work on the pile of rocks again. It hadn't even   166
gone away when it was time to stop for lunch and eat more   179
bananas. By the early afternoon all of the rocks had been   190
removed from the pile.   194

Salt pointed to the bare ground. "The place where the knife   205
handle was is where we start digging."   212

[1]

Everybody dug. Every hour they stopped and rested. They   221
drank water—lots of water. Then they picked up their shovels   232
and dug. The ground was soft and full of bugs and worms.   244
Rosa pulled out a worm that was over three feet long.   255

As they dug down, the soil turned different colors. At first it   267
was black. After they had dug down about a foot, it turned   279
yellow. It stayed yellow for about three feet. Then it turned   290
light gray. The light gray soil was harder than the other soil.   302

Tony was in the hole, digging through the light gray soil. The   314
hole was so deep that Tony could hardly look over the top of it.   328
Salt said, "Stop digging. We're in the wrong place."   337

"What?" Tony said, and he threw down his shovel. "What do 348
you mean?" 350

[1]

Salt said, "The ones who hid this treasure were very clever. 361
They put the trap here, but they didn't put the treasure here." 373

"How do you know?" Rosa asked. "Maybe we'll find it if we 385
keep on digging." 388

"No, no," Salt said. "Look at the sides of your hole. You can 401
see how the soil changes color. That soil has been here for 413
thousands of years. If you threw dirt into a hole, it wouldn't 425
form bands like that. There would be some black dirt at the 437
bottom of the pile. And there would be gray dirt near the top. 450
We're digging in the wrong place." 456

[1]

"Where is the right place?" Tony asked. "This is the place 467
that is marked on the map." 473

"Maybe it is," Salt said. "And maybe this is the place where 485
you find something that marks the treasure if you know what 496
you're looking for." 499

"We found the knife handle," Rosa said. "That shows we're in 510
the right place." 513

Salt said, "Maybe the knife handle tells us where to go. Let's 525
follow the chain and see where it leads us." 534

[1]

Salt pulled on the rusty chain. Chunks of rust fell off as he 547
pulled. He began to follow the chain up the side of the volcano. 560
About thirty feet above the place where the knife handle had 571
been, Salt came to a ledge. He called down, "Here's where the 583
rocks were piled. Throw me a shovel." 590

Tony tossed his shovel. It didn't go up high enough. Rosa   601

tossed her shovel. Salt grabbed it and disappeared. They waited.   611

Then Salt came to the edge of the ledge. He was carrying a   624

shovel full of dirt.   628

[1]

Salt said, "Look at this." He held up a big clump of gray soil.   642

Then he held up a big clump of yellow soil. He dumped the dirt   656

over the ledge. Tony and Rosa bent over the dirt. There was   668

black soil, and yellow soil, and gray soil.   676

"You found it," Rosa said.   681

"That I did," Salt said. He was sweating and smiling. "That I   693

did."   694

Tony and Rosa scrambled up the side of the volcano. Tony   705

remembered to bring his shovel. When they reached the ledge   715

they saw Salt bent over.   720

Without looking up, Salt said, "They put the treasure under   730

the rocks. I don't see any more traps. Let's dig down and see   743

what we find."   746

[1]

Salt pushed the shovel into the ground. "Clink." He tossed   756

the dirt aside. And there it was, the corner of a treasure chest.   769

Tony began to dig. Slowly the dirt was cleared from the   780

chest. It was rusty, and there were a couple of holes in it. Salt   794

put his finger in one of the holes. Then he brought out a round   808

coin. It looked like a black penny.   815

"What's that?" Rosa asked.   819

Salt said, "I'll show you what that is." He rubbed the coin on   832

the leg of his pants. Then he held up the coin. It was shining   846

like the sun. It was bright. IT WAS GOLD.   855

[1]

1

A	B	C	D
beard	charge	drank	tackle
board	change	drunk	tangle

2

know   knot   knife   knew

3

<u>buried</u>   <u>shoulder</u>   <u>iron</u>   reflection

distance   protection   uncovered   scoop

shiny   rough   sparkled   stacked   couple

handfuls   looped   crown   worth   pulled

enough   thought   calm   wrong   swung

drinking   burlap   weighs   gems

brought   wedged   flew   pushed

4

Gold, Gold, Gold

Salt, Rosa, and Tony had found the chest that had been   11
buried on Rose Island. Salt reached inside a hole in the chest   23
and pulled out a gold coin.   29

The top of the chest was uncovered. A large, rusty lock hung   41
from the chest lid. Salt took his shovel and swung it hard. He   54
hit the lock. Bits of rust flew into the air. The lock swung back and   69
forth. Again Salt swung at the lock, and again bits of rust flew into   83
the air. On the third swing, the lock fell to the ground in two pieces.   98

[1]

Salt wedged the scoop of his shovel under the lid of the chest 111
and pushed down. Slowly the lid began to <u>move</u>. Rosa and 122
Tony grabbed the lid and pulled up. The lid opened. For a long 135
moment, they stared into the chest. Nobody said a thing. 145

Tony looked into the chest, and he felt very strange. He 156
could hear himself breathing. In the distance were sounds of 166
jungle birds. His eyes were fixed on what he saw inside the 178
chest. It didn't look the way he had thought it would. 189

[1]

Tony had thought that he would see heaps of shiny coins and 201
gold crowns. He had thought he would see huge red gems that 213
sparkled and gold drinking cups. But he saw heaps of black 224
coins. Some of them were covered with green mold. Some of 235
them had specks of white on them, but most of them were 247
black. 248

There were three or four bugs in the chest, too. They 259
scrambled down between the coins when the chest was opened. 269

"Tony and Rosa," Salt said softly, "we have found the SS 281
Foil's treasure. And what a treasure it is!" 289

[1]

Salt was talking louder and faster. "Do you have any idea 300
how much this treasure must be worth?" He picked up a large 312
coin. "How much do you think this coin is worth?" 322

"Twenty dollars?" Tony asked. 326

"It's more like three hundred dollars," Salt said. "And we 336
have hundreds and hundreds of these coins. We have 345
thousands and thousands. We're rich. We're rich." 352

Salt threw his shovel into the air. Then he began to dance 364
around the chest. He was sweating and singing, "We're rich, 374
Rosa. We're rich, Tony." 378

Rosa joined in. So did Tony. The three of them danced   389
around the chest until they were dizzy.   396

[1]

Tony sat down on the damp ground. Salt was breathing   406
hard. He said, "Now comes the real job of getting the gold out   419
of here."   421

"That chest doesn't look very big," Rosa said. "The three of   432
us could probably carry it."   437

Salt laughed. Then he said, "Let me show you something."   447

He walked to the place where the rope and the other tools   459
were stacked. He picked up a small burlap sack and walked   470
back to the chest. Then he began to fill the sack. When it was   484
full, he handed the sack to Rosa.   491

"Here," Salt said. "See how much a couple of handfuls of   502
gold weighs."   504

[1]

When Rosa grabbed the sack she almost fell over. The sack   515
seemed to pull her to the ground. "Wow," she said. "That sack   527
must weigh fifty pounds."   531

"Let me see," Tony said. He grabbed the sack. It was much   543
smaller than the rocks he and Rosa had moved from the pile,   555
but it seemed to weigh as much as most of them. "Wow," Tony   568
said. "You're right. This stuff weighs more than iron."   577

Salt said, "Yes, gold is much heavier than iron. There aren't   588
many things in this world that weigh as much as gold."   599

[1]

Rosa asked, "Well, how are we going to get the gold out of   612
here?"   613

Salt said, "A little bit at a time. We'll just have to make a lot   628
of trips back to the boat. We'll fill the burlap sacks we brought   641
with us and carry them back to the boat. And we'd better get   654
started right now."   657

Salt went back to the tool pile and came back with three   669
burlap sacks. He said, "Now don't try to fill these sacks all the   682
way, or we won't be able to carry them. Fill them about   694
two-thirds of the way to the top."   701

[1]

Soon three sacks were filled. Then Salt cut three pieces of   712
rope. Each piece was about nine feet long. Then Salt took a   724
piece of rope. He tied both ends around the neck of a sack.   737
Then he looped the rope over one shoulder and around his   748
waist.   749

Salt began to walk. The sack dragged along the ground.   759
"Let's try it this way," Salt said. "I think we won't get as tired if   774
we drag the bags instead of trying to carry them."   784

So Tony tied a piece of rope around a sack. So did Rosa.   797
Then they all began to walk through the jungle, back to the   809
boat.   810

[1]

1

A	B
for	forever
after	afternoon
sun	sunset

2

drenched   breathe   storm   burning

together   shore   hardly   wondered

age   clenched   squall   decided   boiler

3

shoes   figured   dragging   million

probably   through   stones   jungle   rough

done   gem   pulled   rang   buried

charge   engine   iron   calm   pray   easier

spoon   beach   couple   sweat   believe

4

Loading the Boat

Rosa, Tony, and Salt were dragging bags of gold back to the   12
boat. Dragging the sacks through the jungle was not easy. The   23
sacks would drop into little holes. They would catch on the   34
underbrush. At one time Tony thought that it would be easier   45
to lift his sack and carry it. So he carried it for about twenty   59
feet. Then he decided that it would be much easier to drag   71
the sack.   73

Soon Salt and the others were standing at the rim of the hill   86
that led down to the shore. Salt tied the three pieces of rope   99
together. Then he began to let the sacks slide down the side of   112
the hill.   114

[1]

Rosa and Tony scrambled down <u>the</u> hill and held on to the   126
sacks. Then they carried the sacks to the boat.   135

Salt stood up and mopped the sweat from his face. "Look   146
around for some pretty stones," he said. "We'll put them in the   158
sacks. Then if anybody looks into any of the sacks, the person   170
will see stones, not gold."   175

"Good idea," Rosa said.   179

So Rosa and Tony went rock hunting. They found some   189
pretty red stones and some that had streaks of white and   200
yellow in them. They opened the bags and dumped the stones   211
in. Then they tied up the bags and dropped them in the front of   225
the boat.   227

[1]

Salt said, "I think it will take about seven more trips to bring   240
all of the gold down to the boat."   248

"Seven more trips," Rosa said, "Wow. That's going to be   258
rough."   259

Rosa was right. By the time Tony had made three trips, his   271
back was sore. His mouth was dry. And he was drenched with   283
sweat. By the time Tony had made five trips, he could hardly   295
walk. He was in better shape than Rosa. Rosa had to stop and   308
rest every few steps.   312

"The air is so wet I can hardly breathe," she said.   323

[1]

The afternoon sun was beating down on the beach when 333
Salt, Rosa, and Tony came down the hill with the last of the 346
sacks. The sand was so hot that Tony could feel it burning 358
through his shoes. Even Salt was tired. Tony had been thinking 369
that Salt could work forever without stopping. But now he was 380
bent over, dragging the sacks through the soft sand. 389

At last Tony came to the hard, wet sand near the water. He 402
had only a few steps more to go. He filled his last sack with 416
stones. For a moment Tony wondered if he would be able to lift 429
his sack into the boat. He clenched his teeth, closed his eyes, 441
and lifted as hard as he could. 448

[1]

Slowly Tony lifted the sack and let it fall on the other sacks 461
in the nose of the boat. Then he helped Rosa lift her sack into 475
the boat. 477

"Thanks," Rosa said. 480

Salt counted the sacks. "Twenty-four sacks," he said. 488
"Twenty-four sacks." 490

"How much do you think each sack is worth?" Tony asked. 501

"I've got that all figured out. There are about a thousand 512
coins in each sack. That means that each sack is probably 523
worth three hundred thousand dollars." 528

Tony could feel his mouth fall open. The sound of Salt's 539
voice rang in his ear. "Three hundred thousand dollars." 548

[1]

Salt said, "And we have twenty-four sacks, which means that 558
our treasure is worth over seven million dollars." 566

Tony looked at Rosa. Rosa was grinning. Then Rosa hit   576
herself on the head. "I can't believe it. We each have more than   589
two million dollars. I can't believe it."   596

Salt said, "Yes, all we have to do is get that gold back and   610
we'll be rich. Just begin to pray that the sea doesn't decide to   623
take our treasure from us. The sea has done that before. A   635
storm sank the ship that was carrying the treasure. Another   645
storm could take the treasure from us."   652

[1]

"Don't talk that way," Tony said. "We've got the gold, and   663
we're going to get it home. Right, Rosa?"   671

"Right," Rosa said. "If we have to swim home with those   682
sacks, we'll get them home. Right, Salt?"   689

Salt smiled. "Yes. We'll get it home if the sea wants us to   702
take it home. And I hope that the sea does just that. But   715
remember, our boat is going to ride low in the water. There will   728
be nearly 2,000 pounds of weight in the front of the boat. A   741
good squall could send our treasure to the bottom of the   752
ocean. Let's just hope that the sea is calm and that no squalls   765
come up."   767

[2]

1

ra<u>th</u>er   h<u>ou</u>nding   <u>ch</u>oppy

prote<u>ction</u>   slo<u>sh</u>ing   b<u>ai</u>l

h<u>oa</u>rse   bud<u>g</u>e   igni<u>tion</u>

2

<u>above</u>   <u>though</u>   eddies   beginning   shore

shoes   mountains   agreed   measured   reflected

twice   throughout   foggy   muffled

travel   gusts   swung   bucket

steering   decide   waded   pushed   within

tiller   buried   chance   shoulder

3

On the Sea

The sun was setting and the bugs were beginning to come   11
out when Rosa, Tony, and Salt pushed the boat away from the   23
shore. All agreed that it would be better to start back that   35
night than to wait until morning. If they waited until morning,   46
they would have to sleep up on the mountain, far from the   58
boat. If they tried to sleep near the boat, they wouldn't get   70
much sleep, with the bugs hounding them all night. So they   81
agreed that it was best to start their trip back that night.   93

[1]

"Rrr-rrr-rrr," went the starter. "Chu-cug, chu-cug," went the   101
engine. Salt was right. The boat was riding low in the water.   113
Even though Salt had left most <u>of</u> the tools in the jungle, the   126
weight of the gold in the front of the boat was pushing the   139
nose down.   141

Salt, Tony, and Rosa were near the back of the boat. Rosa   153
put her arm over the side and measured the distance from the   165
top of the boat to the water. It was only about a foot. A   179
good-sized wave would wash right into the boat.   187

[1]

But the sea was very calm and the stars were reflected in the   200
water. Rosa said to herself, "Sea, stay calm. Don't get choppy.   211
Just stay calm."   214

And the sea stayed calm throughout the night. Tony slept   224
some, but he kept waking up every time the boat seemed to   236
make a funny move. The air was foggy the next morning, and   248
the sea was still calm. The air seemed heavy and damp. When   260
they talked, their voices sounded muffled. Tony yelled a couple   270
of times just to hear his voice. His voice didn't seem to travel   283
very far in the fog.   288

[1]

Salt said, "There's a chance that the sea will be like this all   301
day. But then there's a chance that a stiff wind will come up   314
and blow the fog away at any time."   322

It wasn't long before they found out what the sea had in store   335
for them. Within an hour, a stiff wind began to blow. At first   348
there were gusts of wind that made eddies across the water.   359
Then the wind began to blow hard and steady. Within a few   371

moments, waves began to form on the ocean. The first waves   382
were small and choppy. These waves soon began to roll into   393
larger and larger waves.   397

[1]

Before long, the waves were rolling and boiling and   406
pounding into the side of the boat. The fog was lifting now,   418
and Tony could see that the ocean was a mass of white,   430
foaming waves. The boat was rocking from side to side as the   442
waves pounded against it. The sound of the waves was very   453
loud.   454

Salt said, "We're going to have to change course. Unless we   465
head into the wind, we'll sink. Those waves will soon be   476
coming over the side of the boat."   483

[1]

Salt swung the boat around so that its nose was headed into   495
the wind. Now the waves were crashing into the front of the   507
boat and sending spray into the air. Tony looked at the bottom   519
of the boat. Already there was water in the boat, sloshing   530
around as the boat rode up and down over the waves.   541

Just then a huge wave hit the front of the boat. It didn't lift   555
the front of the boat the way the other waves did. It came over   569
the front of the boat like a curl of green glass. It seemed to leap   584
inside the boat and —"crash."   589

[1]

The bottom of the boat now had nearly a foot of water in it.   603
The water outside the boat was almost on the same level as the   616
water inside the boat.   620

"We're going down," Rosa yelled above the roar of the   630
waves. "We're sinking."   633

"Bail," Salt yelled in a hoarse voice. "Bail. Grab a bucket— 644
use your hands—use anything. But bail. And don't stop." 654

Another wave crashed against the front of the boat and 664
added about an inch of water. "Bail," Salt yelled. "One more 675
like that, and we're done for." 681

[1]

Tony grabbed a pail and started to throw water from the 692
boat as fast as he could. Rosa was throwing water out with her 705
hands. Salt was using two coffee cans. He was steering the boat 717
by holding his leg against the tiller. 724

"Bail faster," Salt yelled. "Here comes another big one." 733

The wave washed over the front of the boat and sloshed 744
water around inside. Tony said to himself, "This is it. We're 755
going down." But somehow the boat kept floating. 763

Then Salt stood up and waded to the front of the boat. He 776
picked up a sack of gold. 782

"What are you doing?" Tony shouted. 788

"I'm going to save us and the boat," Salt yelled. 798

[1]

1

A	B
motor	motorcycle
through	throughout
out	outside
after	afternoon

2

pail tiller surface stretched

shine chirp engine force

3

pour lose knot hollered above

moment sore seven suddenly

dry allowing rolling million

worried engine few wheezed

sailor trouble minute hungry

knew calm imagine steering

4

Never Make Light of the Sea

    Salt was in the front of the boat. He had just picked up a bag   15
of gold and had told Tony that he was going to do something   28
to save the boat. Salt threw a sack of gold. But he didn't throw   42
it into the ocean. He threw it to the middle of the boat. Then   56
he threw another bag, and another, and another. After he had   67
moved more than ten of the bags, he came back to the tiller.   80

He hollered, "This will put more weight in the back of the 92
boat. The front will be higher in the water. Maybe the waves 104
won't come over it now." 109

[1]

Tony was still bailing. It didn't seem to be doing <u>much</u> to get 122
rid of the water in the bottom of the boat. For every bucketful 135
removed from the boat, a wave added a bucketful. It went on 147
that way for about an hour. 153

The back of the boat was only a little bit above the water. 166
Every now and then it would sink below the surface of the 178
water for a moment, and water would pour in over the back. 190
Every now and then a huge wave would break against the front 202
of the boat and send water flying into the boat. 212

[1]

The boat was climbing up one side of the waves and sliding 224
down the other. At times it seemed to Tony as if the boat was 238
going straight up into the air and then straight down. It was 250
that way for an hour. 255

And then the wind began to die. When the wind stopped, the 267
waves seemed to lose some of their life. They became more 278
rounded. They didn't seem to fight as hard when they struck the 290
boat. They didn't seem to jar the boat with the force they had 303
when the wind was blowing. They didn't seem to move as fast. 315

[1]

Tony and the others were still bailing. They bailed until there 326
was less than an inch of water in the bottom of the boat. Then 340
Rosa said, "Let's stop." 344

"Let's not," Tony said. "We need a big head start on the 356
waves if they're going to start kicking up again. Let's get every 368
drop of water out of this boat." 375

And they did. When they finally stopped bailing, the bottom 385
of the boat was almost dry. 391

Tony sat up straight. His back was sore. He stretched and 402
looked up. The sun was out now. The air was hot and wet. 415
[1]

Salt smiled and began to sing, " 'Tis a sailor's life for me, for 428
me. I sail the seven seas. I go where I go, because I know, this is 444
the life for me." 448

Suddenly he stopped singing and bent forward. "I hope you 458
will remember this. Never make light of the sea. The sea could 470
have had our boat if it wanted to take the boat. It could have 484
taken us if it wanted us. When you pass over the sea, remember 497
that the sea is allowing you to pass." 505
[1]

Everyone was quiet for a long time. The only sound was the 517
"chu-cug, chu-cug" of the engine. From time to time Tony 527
looked at the waves. They were still pretty big, but the boat was 540
rolling over them without any trouble. 546

Tony lay back and closed his eyes. He began to think about 558
the gold. Imagine having two million dollars—two million 567
dollars! What could you buy with all that money? You could 578
buy a motorcycle—five motorcycles. You could buy a boat— 588
any kind of boat you wanted. You could even buy a nice home 601
for your family. You could buy anything you wanted. Wow! 611
[1]

Tony liked to think about these things. But every time he 622
began to feel good about the gold, he remembered what Salt 633
had said and became a little worried about the sea. Salt had 645
said they wouldn't reach Wake Island until just before 654
morning. They would still be in the boat all afternoon, all 665

evening, and almost all of the night. That was a lot of time. 678
And the sea could change very quickly. 685

Tony opened his eyes and looked around. Rosa was eating a 696
banana. The sun was very hot. 702

[1]

The rest of the day passed very slowly. Each minute seemed 713
like an hour to Tony. Each hour seemed like a day. 724

"Come on," Tony said to himself, "we've got to make it." 735

Time moved slowly until about four o'clock in the afternoon. 745
When it happened, Tony was trying to make up his mind about 757
whether he was hungry enough to eat another banana. He had 768
just about decided he would eat one more—just one more— 779
when the engine went, "Chu-cug, chu—" It wheezed a little and 790
stopped. 791

[1]

1

A	B
some	somewhere
through	throughout
any	anyone

2

<u>magneto</u> <u>sign</u> metal cover system

drifted course watching squinted

touch listening cocked tense darkness

dead white wheel whispered enough

appeared transferred pour

engine ignition imagine edge price

3

The Long Night

The engine had died. Tony and the others were somewhere in 11
the South Pacific Ocean. They were more than a hundred miles 22
from Wake Island. The sea was still rough. The boat was turning 34
sideways and rocking as the waves struck it from the side. 45

"What's wrong?" Tony asked. 49

"I won't know until I look at the engine." Salt removed the 61
metal cover from the engine. The engine looked small and old. 72
Salt bent over it. He grabbed the spark plug. "Hit the starter," 84
he said to Rosa. 88

"Rrr-rrr-rrr." 89

"That's enough," Salt said. "The engine is not getting a 99
spark. Something's wrong with the ignition system." 106

[1]

Salt took out his knife and touched different parts of the 117
engine. Then <u>he</u> shook his head. "The magneto is wet," he said. 129

"What do we do now?" Tony asked. 136

"Wait," Salt said. "The sun is bright and hot. With the cover 148
off the engine, it should dry out in a little while." 159

Salt tried the starter every fifteen minutes. The third time he 170
tried it, the engine started. 175

"Good deal," Tony yelled. "We're on our way again." 184

"Yes we are," Salt said, but he shook his head. 194

"What's wrong?" Tony asked. 198

"We drifted quite a bit while the engine was dead," Salt said. 210
"I just hope we didn't drift too far off course." 220

[1]

Tony didn't sleep that night. Neither did the others. Salt 230
remained at the tiller. Rosa was sitting in the front of the boat 243
now. Tony was in the middle. He was watching Salt's face. The 255
moon was bright, and Tony could see Salt clearly. 264

Tony was watching Salt because Salt seemed to know what 274
was happening. When he squinted and looked off to the east, 285
Tony looked to the east. When Salt cocked his head and 296
seemed to be listening to the sound of the engine, Tony cocked 308
his head and listened. It went on like that throughout most of 320
the night. 322

[1]

Morning was near now. This was the time they were 332
supposed to reach Wake Island. Salt's face was tense. His head 343
moved quickly—looking this way and that way. 351

"We should be seeing lights any time," Salt said. But no lights 363
appeared. Salt looked up at the stars. Then he checked his 374
compass. Then he began to look this way and that way again. 386

"I think I see something," Rosa said from the front of the 398
boat. "Over there." She pointed to the west. 406

[1]

Tony squinted and looked where Rosa was pointing. He 415
looked as hard as his eyes could look, but he didn't see anything. 428

"It's not there now," Rosa said. "But I saw a light over there." 441

The boat moved through the water, and everybody in the 451
boat peered into the darkness. For an instant Tony thought he 462
saw some lights, but then he realized that he was looking at the 475
reflection of a star. 479

Suddenly Salt stood up in the boat. Then he stood on the 491
seat. Then he said, "Wake Island is dead ahead. We'll be there 503
pretty soon." 505

Tony grinned. "Good deal," he yelled. 511

Everybody began to sing and laugh. 517

[1]

It seemed like a long time—a long, long time. But, at last, 530
the boat was pulling up to the dock. 538

Salt leaned forward. "Remember," he said, "not one word 547
about gold. We have sacks of rocks. Remember that." 556

Salt tied the boat to the dock. Then he whispered, "You stay 568
here. I'll get a truck for the gold." 576

Tony and Rosa waited in the boat. Two women came down 587
to the docks and went off in a white boat to fish. A gray dog 602
came near, but when Rosa called, it ran to the other end of the 616
dock and disappeared. 619

[1]

At last Salt returned. He was driving an old truck. It looked 631
like an old mail truck. It had a big sign in the rear window. 645
"For Rent," the sign said. Salt parked the truck next to the 657
boat. Then he, Rosa, and Tony transferred the gold from the 668
boat to the truck. 672

After the truck was loaded, Salt drove the truck and 682
followed a dirt road up a hill near the dock. There were no 695
houses on the hill. Salt pulled off the road and turned off the 708
engine. "We'll sleep here for a while, and then we'll see about 720
going home." 722

Tony and Rosa stretched out on the sacks of gold in the back 735
of the truck. Salt went to sleep behind the wheel. 745

[2]

1

A	B
motor	motorboat
over	overlooking
air	airport
news	newspapers

2

squ<u>all</u>   th<u>ir</u>d   n<u>igh</u>t

l<u>oa</u>ded   p<u>ar</u>ked   invita<u>tio</u>ns

blu<u>sh</u>ing   cl<u>ai</u>m   sec<u>tio</u>n

3

<u>insurance</u>   Los Angeles   zone

ticket   Higgins   officer

customs   statements   true

discovered   fifty   pilot's

fellows   pictures   entire

well-wisher   welcome   shake

bald   delivered   banners

reporters   should   people

4

The Trip Home

Tony and the others slept in the truck. When Tony woke up,   12
the truck was moving. Salt was driving the truck and singing,   23
" 'Tis a sailor's life for me, for me. For I sail the seven seas—"   37

"Where are we going now?" Rosa asked.   44

"To the airport, Rosa, to the airport."   51

Salt parked in front of the airport in a no-parking zone.   62
Then he got out of the truck.   69

"If a cop comes over here," Salt said, "tell him I'll punch   81
him in the nose if he tries to give us a ticket."   93

[1]

"Do you really want us to tell him that?" Rosa asked.   104

"I sure do," Salt said. "Tell it like you mean it. I'll feel a lot   119
better with a cop standing next to this truck."   128

Salt <u>went</u> into the airport. Just then a police car pulled up   140
next to the truck.   144

"Move that truck," the cop said.   150

"We can't," Tony said. "We don't have the keys. But the man   162
who is driving this truck said that he'd punch you in the nose if   176
you gave us a ticket."   181

"He said that, did he?" the cop said. He got out of his car   195
and walked to the front of the truck.   203

[1]

The cop made out a ticket and handed it to Rosa. Then he   216
stood next to the truck and waited. In a few minutes Salt came   229
out of the airport. He was walking with a tall woman.   240

"Hand out one of those bags," Salt said. "Mrs. Higgins   250
wants to see the kind of rocks we found on Rose Island."   262

Tony slid one of the sacks along the floor of the truck. Salt grabbed it. 275 277

He untied it and tossed out the rocks. Mrs. Higgins's eyes seemed to pop out when she looked inside the sack. 288 298

"Yes," Salt said, "we've got twenty-four sacks like that one." 308

[1]

"What's going on here?" the cop demanded. 315

Mrs. Higgins said, "I think it's all right, officer. These people have found the *Foil* treasure." 326 331

"They did what?" The cop asked. 337

Mrs. Higgins pulled a handful of gold coins from the sack and showed them to the cop. The cop's eyes seemed to pop. "Are those gold coins?" he asked. 348 360 366

"Thousands and thousands of them," Salt said. 373

Salt, Tony, and Rosa spent most of the day filling out papers and talking to people. They filled out papers for insurance. They filled out papers to claim the gold. They talked to people from the newspapers. And they talked to Mrs. Higgins. 385 395 407 416

[1]

Mrs. Higgins was a customs officer. She wrote out the entire story of how Salt, Tony, and Rosa had discovered the gold. Then Salt, Rosa, and Tony filled out statements saying that the report was true. Mrs. Higgins told them the gold would be delivered to a bank in their home town. 427 438 449 460 468

That night, Salt, Tony, and Rosa stayed in a fine hotel overlooking the beach on Wake Island. Tony slept like a log. In the morning he ate eggs and toast and lots of juice. But he didn't eat one banana. 479 491 504 508

[1]

Later a big black car took them to the airport. They were to 521
fly back on a jumbo jet. 527

They sat in the first-class section of the plane. After the plane 539
was in the air, the pilot's voice came over the loudspeaker. "We are 552
glad to have three very happy people with us today. These people 564
have done something that many others have tried to do over the 576
last fifty years. They found the *Foil* treasure. The word that I have 589
is that the treasure is worth about seven million dollars." 599

[1]

The people in the plane went, "Ooo," and, "Ahhh," and, 609
"Wow!" Some of them clapped. Tony felt himself blushing. 618

The flight back home didn't seem to take much time. Tony 629
remembered the days he had worked in the boiler room on the 641
ship that went to Wake Island. The jumbo jet made it across 653
the ocean in less than 12 hours. 660

Reporters met the plane when it landed in Los Angeles. 670
They asked many questions, and they took pictures. They 679
invited Salt, Rosa, and Tony to have lunch with them. 689

[1]

The next day the three arrived home. Again they were met by 701
reporters and questions and pictures and invitations for lunch 710
and dinner. People were waving and yelling. They were holding 720
up banners that said, "Welcome home, Tony and Rosa." 729

There were no banners to welcome Salt home. But the reporters 740
seemed to like to talk to Salt. They asked him most of the questions. 754

Then the last question had been asked, the last handshake 764
was over, and the last well-wisher had left. Tony, Rosa, and 775
their mom and dad went home. Their mom cried a little bit, 787
but they could see that she was very happy and very proud. 799

[1]

1

A	B
news	newspaper
under	understand
gentle	gentleman
in	indeed

2

<u>graduated</u> <u>guess</u> accounts sixteen tossed

stole eight blinked interested

figuring lonely adventure tomorrow

forward world friends ashamed

barked watch invitation insurance

range police officer advice brought

3

Salt's Real Treasure

The day after Salt and the others came home, Tony was 11
reading accounts of the treasure hunt in the newspaper. One 21
account said that they came back with sixteen bags of gold. 32

"That's not right," Tony said. 37

He glanced through another account. It said the same thing. 47
It said that Salt and Tony and Rosa had found twenty-four 58
sacks but brought back only sixteen. 64

The account said, "When Salt was asked what happened to 74
the other sacks, he said, 'They went back to the sea.'" 85

Tony tossed the newspaper aside. He got Rosa and they ran   96
from the house. They ran all the way to Salt's house. Salt was   109
sitting on the front steps talking to three people.   118

[1]

Tony said, "Salt, can we go inside? We want to ask <u>you</u>   130
something."   131

"Sure," Salt said.   134

So Tony, Rosa, and Salt went inside. They went upstairs to   145
Salt's room. It seemed to Tony that it was a hundred years ago   158
when they had been in that room before, looking at the map,   170
trying to figure out how to crack the code.   179

Tony asked, "How many bags did we bring back?"   188

"I can see it in your face," Salt said. "You're thinking that   200
Old Salt stole some of your gold. No, my boy, you have your   213
eight bags, and Rosa has her eight bags."   221

[1]

Tony asked again, "How many bags did we bring back?"   231

"Twenty-four bags," Salt said.   235

Rosa said, "But the newspaper said we brought back only   245
sixteen bags. Where are your eight bags?"   252

"Where they should be," Salt said.   258

Tony looked at Rosa and blinked. Salt walked over to the   269
desk picture of his captain. "Who led us to the gold?"   280

Rosa pointed to the picture. "I guess he did," Rosa said.   291

"Indeed he did," Salt said. "He sent us the trunk. And that   303
trunk is what got you interested. Then he gave us the map. And   316
then maybe he even gave us a little help in figuring out how to   330
break the code."   333

[1]

Tony said, "But he's dead. You can't pay him back." 343

"Oh, can't I?" Salt said and laughed. "My captain spent his 354
last days in a home for old sailors. The days of an old sailor 368
can be lonely, or they can be like a golden sunset. I think that 382
my captain would want me to do something for that sailors' 393
home. After all, the map came from the sailors' home." 403

Rosa asked, "Did you give all your treasure to that sailors' 414
home?" 415

"No, Rosa," Salt said. "I didn't give them any of my treasure. 427
I gave them nothing but gold. Eight tired little bags of gold. I 440
kept the treasure for myself." 445

[1]

"What are you talking about?" Tony asked. "You gave them 455
the gold—that's the treasure." 460

"No, no," Salt said. "The treasure was the adventure. You 470
can't understand this because you're young, and you have your 480
life in front of you. But for me, there were no plans. Tomorrow 493
wasn't a thing I looked forward to. It was something I knew 505
would come, and I knew it would be like the day before." 517

"But then I found the greatest treasure of them all. I had a 530
chance to be young again. Like a fool, I could make plans and 543
dream of gold. I had two friends, and together we would go 555
halfway around the world. That was the treasure. The gold was 566
the reason, but the real treasure was you and Rosa and the 578
days we spent together." 582

[2]

Both Rosa and Tony looked at Old Salt. Tony felt very sad 594
and ashamed. He said, "I see what you mean. We had some 606
time, didn't we? I guess I'll remember that trip for the rest of 619
my life." 621

"Me, too," Rosa said. "But what are you going to do for   633
money, Salt?"   635

Salt stood up and waved his arms around. "I have this house.   647
And how much money does an old man need? I suppose I'll   659
spend most of my time sitting on the porch. Maybe I'll take a   672
little trip once in a while. But I don't need much money. Besides,   685
the sailors' home can make better use of that gold than I can."   698

Rosa said, "Do you think Tony and I should give some of   710
our gold away?"   713

"No," Salt barked. "That gold is yours. You keep it and   724
make good use of it. Just don't let it change your life.   736
Remember, the gold is not the real treasure. The real treasure   747
is the treasure hunt. The treasure is doing things and having   758
good friends with you."   762

[1]

Tony remembered what Salt said. He remembered it for   771
years and tried to follow the advice that Salt had given him.   783
Tony didn't buy a lot of motorcycles and cars. He didn't act as   796
if he were a big-timer. He and Rosa helped their mother and   808
father buy a new house. Tony went back to school, and he   820
worked hard. After he graduated, he went on to college and   831
worked hard. Whenever he had a chance, he went to visit Old   843
Salt. And once each year during the summer, Tony, Rosa, and   854
Old Salt got together and talked about their adventure.   863

One more thing happened. After that adventure, nobody   871
made fun of Old Salt.   876

[1]

1

A	B
drive	driveway
over	overlooking
birth	birthday

2

trout   gear   loaded   partner   sailors

entertainment   sneakiest   treatment

ostrich   whoop   dirty   couches

reformed   surprise   whale

3

received   New Bedford   Emma

bluff   Charlie   assistant

banged   event   howled   corporal

ahoy   laughter   graduated   folks

4

A Surprise Party

It was Salt's birthday, so Rosa and Tony decided to throw a   12
big party at the old sailors' home. Rosa and Tony wanted to   24
surprise Salt, so they didn't tell him about the party. But they   36
tried to invite all of the people that he had talked about.   48

He had once talked about a rancher named Emma Branch,   58
so they invited her. One time Salt had told a tale about a funny   72
con man, so they invited him. And of course they invited all of   85

the old people who lived in the home—men and women who   97
had spent their lives sailing and fishing.   104
[1]

On the day of the party, Rosa and Tony went over to Salt's   117
home. They pulled up in Rosa's car. "Salt," they called, "let's   128
go <u>for</u> a little outing."   133

Salt said, "I'm ready for an outing. I thought I would go   145
down to the stream and see if I could catch some trout."   157

"We wanted to go for a drive," Rosa said. "But why don't   169
you bring your fishing gear along? We may find a place to do   182
some fishing."   184

So Old Salt loaded his gear into the car, and the car took off   198
down the street.   201
[1]

It was nearly a hundred miles to the old sailors' home. When   213
Salt, Rosa, and Tony had gone over sixty miles, Salt said,   224
"Where are we going?"   228

"We thought we'd stop off at New Bedford," Tony said.   238

"That's where the sailors' home is," Salt said. "Could we stop   249
by there to say hello?"   254

"Sure," Rosa said. She and Tony smiled.   261

Salt directed them to the sailors' home. It was on a large   273
bluff overlooking the sea. It was a big place with lots of rooms.   286
Rosa parked the car in a driveway in front of the white house.   299
[1]

Salt got out of the car and stretched. Then he yelled, "Ahoy,   311
there. Is anybody home?"   315

Nobody answered. Salt said, "Those folks must be hard of   325
hearing. Let's go in and wake them up."   333

Salt, Rosa, and Tony went up the front steps and inside the 345
building. It was dark in the huge living room. And it was very 358
quiet. 359

"Where is everybody?" Salt barked. 364

Just then somebody snapped on the lights. Somebody opened 373
the drapes. And everybody yelled, "Surprise! Surprise!" 380

Old sailors jumped up from behind couches and chairs. They 390
popped out from behind the drapes and from behind the 400
doors. They walked across the floor, yelling and laughing and 410
slapping Salt on the back. 415

[1]

"You're a sight for sore eyes," the old sailors said to Salt. 427

For a few moments Salt stood there with his mouth open and 439
his eyes wide. Then he began to yell and whoop it up. 451

"Charlie!" he yelled, and hugged one of the old sailors. "You 462
old bum," Salt said. "I thought we saw you for the last time in 476
South America." 478

Charlie tried to tell Salt how he got out of South America after 491
the ship had sailed without him. But Salt couldn't hear what 502
Charlie was saying. Other people were grabbing Salt, slapping 511
him, jumping up and down, and having a whale of a time. 523

[1]

The rancher came out of the crowd. She picked Salt up and 535
swung him around. "Good seeing you, you dirty old goat," 545
Emma said. 547

"Put me down," Salt yelled. So the rancher dropped him on 558
his seat in the middle of the floor. He shook his fist, and his 572
face turned red. All the old people and the rancher howled 583
with laughter. 585

Just then a man walked in the room. He was leading another 597
man. He stopped in the middle of the floor. He said, "I am in 611
charge of the entertainment. My assistant and I have lots of 622
fun and games planned for everybody." 628

Old Salt said, "I don't know that fellow who's talking, but I 640
know his assistant. He's the sneakiest sneak in the South 650
Pacific—the con man himself." 655

[1]

The con man took a bow. The other man, the president, said, 667
"I'll have you know that my assistant is a reformed man. He 679
has received treatment at the Happy Hollow Rest Home. Isn't 689
that right, corporal?" 692

"Yes," the con man said. 697

Everybody clapped. Some of the old people banged their 706
canes on the floor. 710

"Our first event," the president said, "will be an 719
egg-throwing contest. The rules are simple. You pick a partner. 729
You stand two steps from your partner. You throw the egg. If 741
your partner catches it without breaking it, each of you takes 752
one big step backward. This keeps up until we have a winner." 764

"What happens if we break an egg?" one old woman asked. 775

"We pick you up and throw you off the dock," the president 787
said. "But if you and your partner win, we have a fine prize for 801
you. Everybody, go outside, and we'll line up for the game." 812

[2]

1

A	B	C	D	E
throw	woman	stream	drive	anybody
threw	women	scream	drove	nobody

2

ran<u>ch</u>er l<u>oa</u>ded <u>p</u>artners str<u>ea</u>m

ca<u>tch</u> h<u>ea</u>ring spla<u>sh</u> bun<u>ch</u>

l<u>ea</u>ding entert<u>ai</u>nment sn<u>ea</u>kiest

3

<u>c</u>a<u>ugh</u>t argue arguing pairs

silence basket ostrich blamed

splat lousy heave-ho shaking

ladies gentlemen pie-eating

surrounded battling rooms

4

The Egg-Throwing Contest

Salt, Rosa, the rancher, and everybody else ran outside. Salt [10] and Emma Branch were partners. Rosa and Tony were [19] partners. All of the old sailors paired off. Some of them were [31] laughing and horsing around. [35]

"Silence," the president said. "We must have silence." [43]

Everybody became quiet and looked at the president. Next [52] to him was a huge basket. [58]

"To make the game more interesting, we have large eggs," [68] the president said. [71]

Salt said, "Those are ostrich eggs. They are bigger than [81] baseballs." [82]

The con man passed out the eggs. The old folks laughed and   94
talked with each other.   98

"Silence," the president said. "Everybody, line up and begin   107
the game. Throw your eggs."   112

[1]

There were about thirty pairs of people playing the game.   122
The eggs went into the air. Everybody <u>caught</u> the eggs except   133
one man named Stan. His egg landed on his shirt with a   145
"splat." Everybody but that man and his partner laughed.   154

Stan, the man who missed the egg, was madder than   164
someone covered with cotton-taffy pike. He said to his partner,   174
"Pete, you didn't have to throw a line drive at me."   185

"Line drive, my foot," Pete said. "If you had put your glasses   197
on, you might have caught that egg."   204

"Pete," said Stan, "that was a lousy toss."   212

[1]

The partners kept arguing. Even as the con man and the   223
president picked them up and gave them the heave-ho into the   234
water, they kept arguing.   238

The game went on. Everybody took one more step back.   248

"Everybody, throw your eggs." Everybody caught the eggs.   256

"Take one big step back," the president said. "Throw your eggs."   267

This time two people missed. Both of them blamed the ones   278
who threw the eggs. "Don't throw me in the water," one old   290
man said. "It was that bum. He couldn't hit the side of a barn if   305
he was locked inside."   309

"Splash!" Off the end of the dock the partners went.   319

[1]

The game went on. Soon there were only four pairs of   330
partners left in the game. They were surrounded by people who   341

were dripping wet and yelling and shouting, "Come on, toss   351
those eggs," and, "You're going to miss your egg."   360

When the partners were twenty steps apart, Tony missed his   370
egg. Rosa threw it short, and Tony made a diving catch. But when   383
he hit the ground—"splat"—ostrich egg went all over the place.   395

The others picked him up and threw him off the end of the   408
dock. Then they threw Rosa in, too.   415

Now there were three pairs left. Emma Branch and Old Salt   426
were still in the contest.   431

[1]

"Come on, Salt," the rancher said. "We can beat the rest of   443
these bums."   445

The people began to yell, "No rancher can beat a sailor.   456
Come on, beat that rancher."   461

The eggs went into the air. Emma caught the egg thrown by   473
Salt, but—"splat!"—it broke. Within two seconds, everyone   482
grabbed the rancher and Salt.   487

"Splash! Splash!" They went into the water.   494

"Somebody's going to pay for this," the rancher said. She   504
was sitting in the water, shaking her fist. One old man laughed   516
so hard that he fell off the end of the dock.   527

[1]

One woman pushed a man off the dock. Then another man   538
pushed Rosa. Then Tony pushed that man. Within a few   548
minutes, everyone was in the water.   554

"Stop this horsing around," the president shouted. "The   562
game is not over yet."   567

Two pairs of old sailors were battling it out for the prize.   579
They tossed the eggs. One old man missed. He jumped up and   591
down and started to shout. But before he could say twenty   602

words, he and his partner were in the water.   611

At last there was a winning team. Each old sailor on the   623
winning team received a live, full-sized ostrich.   630

[1]

"Our next event," said the president, "will be a pie-eating   640
contest. For this event we have set up a long table on the other   654
side of the house. If you will follow me, ladies and gentlemen."   666

Everybody went to the other side of the house. The president   677
pointed to a banana cream pie. "Now you must remember that   688
this is a pie-eating contest. Let me go over the rules with you."   701

The president snapped his fingers, and the con man ran up to   713
him. The president said, "In a pie-eating contest, you may not do   725
this." He picked up the pie and heaved it into the con man's face.   739

"Splat!" The con man's face looked like a big puff of   750
whipped cream.   752

[1]

"Also," the president said, "You may not do this." The president   763
placed a pie on the table in front of the con man. Then he grabbed   778
the con man by the back of the neck and pushed his face into the pie.   794

"That is against the rules," the president said.   802

Salt picked up a pie. He said, "Is this fair?" He tossed the pie   816
and hit the rancher right in the face. "Splat!"   825

"No," the president said. "That is not fair."   833

Suddenly many pies were flying through the air. The   842
president jumped up on the table. "We must have silence," he   853
said. "We must have—"   857

"Splat!" Two pies hit him at the same time. Then many   868
sticky hands grabbed him, lifted him from the table, carried   878
him to the end of the dock, and—"splash!"   887

[1]

1

A	B
tooth	toothpick
night	nightmare
birth	birthday

2

pie-eating   cheered   heap

worth   sneak   pairs   around

dreams   lousy   person   giant

3

put   putting   brought   flying   sore

laughing   glub   finished   glump

sticky   chump   turkey   dragged

hollered   clothes   treasure   ticket

twelve   shoes   belt   feeding

4

The Sale

   Salt was having a surprise party. Pies were flying, people   10
were being tossed into the water, and everybody was getting   20
sore sides from laughing so hard.   26
   The old people had tossed the president into the water.   36
"Please," the president said, "we must have a little order."   46
   The president went back to the table and again explained the   57
rules of the pie-eating contest. The con man brought out   67
another load of pies, and the contest began.   75

"Glub, glump, chump, chump." Everybody ate pie and more   84
pie. Pretty soon a very fat man said, "That's all. I'm finished. I   97
hate pie." Everybody laughed.   101

[1]

The president spotted one person feeding pie to a dog under   112
the table. A woman was trying to feed her pie to an ostrich, but   126
the ostrich didn't <u>like</u> the pie. The ostrich liked a button on the   139
woman's coat.   141

"Get out of here, you giant turkey," the woman yelled.   151

The winner of the pie-eating contest was a tall, slim man   162
named Thin Jim. After everybody else quit, Thin Jim was still   173
putting pie away. "I'm just getting down to my all-day pace. I   185
could eat like this for days. I can eat more than anyone in these   199
parts. I can eat more than—"   205

"Splat!" Three pies hit him at the same time.   214

[1]

Then many sticky hands picked up Thin Jim and pulled him   225
from the table. They dragged him across the grass. They got   236
him to the dock. "Splash!"   241

When Jim came out of the water he said, "You are just mad   254
because I won the pie-eating contest."   260

"So you did," the president said. "And here is the first prize: 272
a gold toothpick."   275

Everybody cheered and clapped as the president handed the   284
prize to Thin Jim. Jim held up the toothpick so that all could see it.   299

"Silence, silence," the president hollered.   304

[1]

The president said, "Our next event is the sale. For this   315
event, you have to bid for things I place on the block.   327
Everybody has three chips. But if you want to bet more than   339

230   *Lesson 64*

three chips, you can bet your clothes. Each piece of clothing is 351
worth one chip. A sock is worth one chip. So is a shoe." 364

One of the old people began to sneak inside the house. "No, 376
you don't," the president shouted. "You must play with the clothes 387
you have on. You can't sneak inside and put on a heap of clothes." 401

"This isn't fair," one sailor yelled. "Fuzz always wears three 411
pairs of socks. That isn't fair." 417

[1]

"What do you mean it isn't fair?" Fuzz said. "I can't help it if 431
I got jungle sickness. It was in the summer of sixty-three. We 443
were near Wake Island when our ship—" 450

"Splat!" The president had thrown that pie. Several people 459
picked Fuzz up and tossed him off the end of the dock. 471

"Let's begin the sale." The president snapped his fingers, and the 482
con man came out with a large box. The president pointed to the 495
box. "Here it is, ladies and gentlemen. Inside this box you might 507
find a treasure or a turkey. It may be the wish of your dreams or a 523
nightmare. What do you bid for this box and everything inside it?" 535

[1]

"Wait a minute," Thin Jim yelled. "How can we bid if we 547
can't see what's in the box?" 553

"My good man," the president said, "if you don't wish to join 565
in this sale, just step to the back of the crowd and give your 579
three chips to your friends. But if you choose to stay and bid, 592
you won't know what's inside a box until it is opened." 603

"Come on, give me your chips," said a woman next to Jim. 615

"Get out of here," Jim said. "I'm staying, and I'm bidding. I 627
bid one chip." 630

"Two chips," yelled Stan, the man who had dropped the first egg. 642

[1]

The president began to call, "I've got a bid for two, two, two, 655
and who'll make it three, three, three? Who'll make it three?" 666

"Three," the rancher yelled. 670

"Four," yelled Stan. He was sitting down, taking off his shoe. 681

The president called, "He's got a four, four, four. Who's 691
going for a five, five, five? That's it. All done. Sold to the man 705
for four. Get them in; get them out. Let's go." 715

The con man ran over to Stan, handed him the box, and 727
picked up the three chips and one shoe. Everybody crowded 737
around as Stan opened the box. He reached inside and held up 749
a baseball mitt. 752

"That's just what I need," he said. He sat down and put the 765
mitt on his foot. "And to think I gave up a good shoe for this," 780
he said. 782

[1]

The next box on sale went for three chips. Inside was a ticket 795
that was good for twelve flying lessons. The next box went for 807
five—two shoes, two socks, and one belt. Inside were two 818
tickets to a baseball game. 823

The sailor who got that box was very mad. "And to think I gave 837
up my clothes for two lousy baseball tickets," the sailor yelled. 848

Then the con man dragged out a box that was almost as big 861
as he was. The bidding started. The rancher took off both her 873
shoes and socks and her hat. "I'll bid eight," Emma said. 884

Thin Jim bid nine—three chips, two shoes, two socks, one 895
shirt, and one belt. 899

Someone in the back yelled, "I bid ten." 907

[1]

1

A	B	C	D
ten	bubble	teeth	gasped
tin	babble	tooth	grasped

2

undershorts   around   float   hooray

watermelon   hollered   turtle   shirt

3

howling   laughter   comic   false   lovely

listening   magician   invisible   experiment

pillow   fingers   choke   lungs   mirror

4

The End

"I bid ten," Fuzz yelled, holding up three chips, a shoe, and   12
his three pairs of socks.   17

Everyone around him was howling and cheering. "Going,   25
going," the president yelled. "Gone to the man in the back."   36

Fuzz ran up and grabbed the box. He ripped it open. Inside   48
was a comic book and sixty sticks of bubble gum.   58

"I can't chew this," Fuzz yelled. "It pulls out my false teeth."   70
He passed the bubble gum around to the other people. They   81
were blowing bubbles and getting gum all over their faces.   91

"That ends the sale," the president said. "But there is one last   103
event, this—"   105

"Splat!" That was the last of the cream pies.   114

[1]

"This kind of horsing around will have to stop," the   124
president yelled.   126

Nobody was listening to him. They were watching Pete. He   136
was blowing a bubble as big as a watermelon. Then somebody   147
broke it. Pete had a mask of gum.   155

"Our final event," the president said, "is Irma the Fantastic."   165

Everybody clapped. Someone said, "Who's that?"   171

"Don't you know?" a sailor said. "She's the most fantastic   181
magician in the world."   185

"Where is she?" a man yelled.   191

"She's standing right next to me," the president said.   200

"She isn't, either," the man yelled.   206

[1]

Just then, one of the socks that had been bid in the sale   219
began to float in the air. Then it seemed to slide onto a foot.   233
The other sock floated onto another foot. Then a pair of pants   245
seemed to slide onto an invisible body. Then a shirt went on   257
the invisible body.   260

Now the whole body was visible, except for the head and the   272
hands. The body walked toward the rancher. Slowly an   281
invisible hand took the rancher's hat and placed it on the   292
invisible head.   294

One man shouted, "Do you see what I see?"   303

The people clapped and yelled. Irma slowly took off the   313
clothes. Then she rubbed some oil on her face. As she rubbed   325
her face it slowly became visible. All anyone could see was a   337
face floating in the air.   342

[1]

Irma said, "I'm going to do a trick I've never done before.   354
I'm going to make somebody else invisible. Since it's Salt's   364

birthday, I'm going to experiment on him. I sure hope it 375
works." 376

Everyone laughed and began to push Salt toward Irma. "Get 386
your hands off me," Salt hollered. 392

Irma looked at Salt and frowned. "Since this is the first time 404
I've made anybody else invisible, I don't think I'll make every 415
part of him invisible. I think I'll just do half his face." 427

[1]

She held a bit of invisible paint in her hand. She rubbed her 440
hand up and down over the right half of Salt's face. As she 453
rubbed, she said, "Oh, power of powers, make his face invisible." 464

Then she stopped and shook her head. "I'm glad I didn't try 476
this trick in my act," she said. "As you can see, it isn't working. 490
Thank you anyhow, Salt. It looks like you're just not the 501
invisible type." 503

"I never did trust magicians," Salt said. 510

Irma said, "But maybe you can help me with another trick." 521
She handed him a pillow case. "Would you put this all the way 534
over your head?" 537

"No, I don't—" 540

[1]

Before Salt could say anything more, Herman was helping 549
Salt put the case over his head. Irma said to the people, "For 562
my next trick, I'm going to change Salt into a lovely turtle. 574
When I snap my fingers, he will become a little green turtle." 586

"I will not," Salt said. He jerked the pillow case from his head. 599

Half his face was invisible. Everybody gasped and went, "Ohhh." 609

Irma handed Salt a mirror. Salt stared into the mirror. He 620
started to say something, but he stopped. He just stared. 630

[1]

Irma said, "Oh, my. I didn't think it would work." 640
Everybody except Salt laughed. Irma said, "I just wish I could 651
remember how to make him visible." 657

Finally, Irma came over with an oil rag and wiped his face. 669
Slowly it became visible. 673

"I never did trust magicians," Salt said. "But glad I am that 685
you made my face visible again." 691

Tony, Rosa, Salt, and everybody else had a big dinner. Then 702
they sat around a large fire outside and sang old songs of the 715
sea. And then it was time for Salt, Tony, and Rosa to go. 728

Suddenly all the people stopped joking around. Everything 736
was quiet, except for the sound of logs on the fire. 747
[1]

Then Thin Jim said, "We all want to thank you, Salt. It's 759
your birthday, but we're the ones who had the party. We used 771
to be a bunch of old people, just sitting around here. But you 784
showed us that we can still laugh and have a good time. We've 797
got a lot of fun left in us. We—" 806

Thin Jim began to choke. He had tears in his eyes. 817

Someone yelled, "Let's hear it for Salt. Hip, hip, hooray! Hip, 828
hip, hooray! Hip, hip, hooray!" 833

Tony never forgot the sound of those people yelling "Hip, 843
hip, hooray" at the top of their lungs. He never forgot the look 856
of joy in their eyes. At one time he had thought that old people 870
were funny, but he didn't feel that way any more. 880

THIS IS THE VERY END. 885
[1]